Los Angeles Jew

A Memoir

Martin Aaron Brower

authorHOUSE®

AuthorHouse™
1663 Liberty Drive, Suite 200
Bloomington, IN 47403
www.authorhouse.com
Phone: 1-800-839-8640

First published by AuthorHouse 3/27/2009

ISBN: 978-1-4389-5520-9 (sc)
ISBN: 978-1-4389-5521-6 (hc)

Library of Congress Control Number: 2009902326

Printed in the United States of America
Bloomington, Indiana

This book is printed on acid-free paper.

To Tamar, who brought her special smile
from Baltimore to Los Angeles,
and to Steve, Dan, Judy and Marla,
who -- like me -- are native Angelenos

Contents

Introduction

In 1928, the year in which I was born in the City of Los Angeles, the City's population of 1,200,000 persons included 65,000 Jews, a mere footnote in the annals of world Jewish population.

In 2008, the year in which I wrote this memoir, the City of Los Angeles' population of 3,800,000 includes 520,000 Jews, a number exceeded only by New York City and Tel Aviv, Israel.

Although countless novels and non-fiction books have described in grand detail the development of Jewish life in New York City to the greatest extent, and Chicago, Philadelphia and areas of New Jersey to a lesser extent, little – in fact nearly nothing -- has been written about the experience of Los Angeles Jews as their community underwent its amazing growth.

Certainly the experiences of growing up in New York's lower east side, then in Brooklyn and the Bronx, and later on Long Island are significant. But the experiences of growing up in Los Angeles, from the original Jewish enclave of Boyle Heights on the east side into the ambiance of West Los Angeles, the San Fernando Valley and beyond, was an entirely different experience from that of the Eastern and Midwestern cities.

As a journalist, I have long planned to complete a definitive generational novel based on the Los Angeles Jewish experience. And such a novel has been underway for many years. But the novel form is a difficult one for a journalist, and the completion is far into the future. For that reason, I decided to undertake a personal memoir to capture what I believe to be the unique Jewish Los Angeles experience.

In doing so, it is necessary to point out that my Jewish life during my early years of growing up in Los Angeles was somewhat different from the mainstream. Unlike the young Los Angeles Jews whose fathers excelled economically through wholesaling, retailing, manufacturing, distribution, homebuilding or indeed the motion picture industry, my father was a workingman who struggled through the depression and earned a comfortable but relatively lower-income living thereafter. As a result, my early and teenage years were spent in a lower-income, non-Jewish section of Los Angeles. Those same years spent in the more affluent Jewish sections of the City would have yielded a somewhat different initial experience.

However, in later years, attending the then heavily-Jewish University of California at Los Angeles, living on the heavily-Jewish west side of Los Angeles and becoming acquainted with those who did grow up in these areas, I have attempted to reflect that early golden opportunity.

Then, based on my career as a journalistic and public relations professional associated as an insider with a number of organizations and firms intimately connected with all of Los Angeles and Southern California, I believe that I am well-qualified to present the unique and exciting Los Angeles Jewish experience through my life and first-hand observations.

Prologue

They sat in the elegant sanctuary of the Reform Jewish congregation, row-upon-row of men and women in their 50s and 60s. They were well-dressed, well-coiffed, and exuded the subtle scents of fine perfumes and masculine colognes. Only half-listening to the rabbi, they stole glances around the room. Anticipating. Hoping. And even silently praying.

At their sides sat young men and women aged 18 to 25. The young men were equally well dressed, a finely trimmed beard here and there, lots of mustaches. Handsome. Well mannered. The young women, perhaps overdressed for the Friday evening services, were stylish to the moment. Beautiful.

The young people also sat only half-listening to the rabbi. They wanted to steal sideward glances, but most did not dare give in to the impulse. Half anticipating. Half bored. Fully cool.

They had come because their parents had insisted – and because they were mildly curious. To an extent, every young man did sort of want to meet a Jewish girl. And every young lady would kind of have liked to please her mother and meet a nice Jewish boy. Parents sat on the edge of their seats.

Following the hour-long worship service, the congregation reassembled in the spacious social hall. Some of the young people nibbled at the cookies and cakes. A few chatted rather formally with friends met several years earlier at the temple's religious school. Others stood awkwardly with their parents, enduring introductions to their parents' friends.

As if on a timer, formalities over and the requisite 20 minutes of socializing concluded, the young people began moving individually to the exits. They had come in their own cars so that they could escape early without having to wait for their parents.

This was college homecoming night 2008 at the fashionable Reform Jewish temple atop a high summit in Los Angeles' Santa Monica Mountains just off the 405 Freeway and Mulholland Drive, with views of the heavily Jewish Beverly Hills and West Los Angeles on one side and of the heavily Jewish Encino and the rest of the San Fernando Valley on the other. Adjacent to the huge temple was the massive campus of the American Jewish University. A few blocks along Mulholland to the west was the impressive Michael Milken Jewish Community High School. And across the 405 from the temple was the stately Skirball Center, a world-class Jewish museum.

The evening had been scheduled to coincide with the brief visit home of the college students during the winter recess. And as eagerly as the parents had waited for the evening to arrive, just as eagerly had their sons and daughters waited to depart.

The college students slid into their expensive Japanese and German sports cars, turned on a heavy metal audio disc with relief, and fled into the cool, star-filled Southern California night.

Chapter One: From Latvia to Los Angeles via Cleveland

The Lure of Los Angeles

My father was lured to Los Angeles from Cleveland in 1925. He was literally seduced by the Los Angeles Chamber of Commerce which in the early 1920s promised sunshine, orange trees and the opportunity for personal and financial growth in advertisements placed in the newspapers of cold, snowy and long-settled Cleveland.

You could say that my father was an adventurer. Born Yankel Beryl Brower in the City of Mitau in the Kurland region of Latvia in 1896, as the eldest of then-five children he willingly left his parents' struggling home at the age of six to live with his adoring grandparents, was apprenticed to a tinsmith at the age of nine, and then left his small town as a teenager to make his fortune as a sheet metal man in the big city of Riga He was tall for those years, light complected, a good conversationalist, and handsome.

Word of golden opportunities in the United States of America fired his interest in America. His father, Benjamin, had visited the United States, enjoyed a visit with a sister in Kalamazoo, Michigan, and rather than sending for his family, returned home.

So in 1913, at the age of 17, my father Yankel was off by himself to Kalamazoo to stay with his aunt and make his fortune. In Kalamazoo, Yankel became Jack.

Although he had little education and spoke no English, Jack soon found work in that city as a sheet metal man for $6 a week. From his pay envelope he gave his aunt $4 a week for room and board, saved $1 a week to bring his father to America, and used the remaining single dollar for lunch, clothes and incidental expenses. By 1914 he was able to bring his father to join him.

When his new country, America, went to war in 1917, Jack enlisted in the U.S. Army and this automatically gave him U.S. citizenship, in which he took great pride. To his dismay, the war ended before he could be sent overseas to fight the Germans and he was discharged in 1919.

On discharge from the Army, he returned to work as a sheet metal man in several small Ohio cities, where he became a coveted sheet metal journeyman. While Jack was in the Army, his father had also worked as a sheet metal man, and together they decided to open their own sheet metal shop in the big city of Cleveland.

As the business grew -- and contrary to the wishes of my grandfather who felt that life was good without the rest of the family -- in 1921 my father brought his entire family to America: mother Ida, sisters Bessie, Shirley and Thelma, and brothers Marvin and baby Harry.

Life in Cleveland was now satisfying for Jack, but advertisements in local newspapers promoting the golden promise of Los Angeles continued to seduce him. The stories and pictures he had seen had fired his curiosity to experience and to conquer this land of sunshine, oranges and opportunity.

So at the age of 29, my father decided to visit Los Angeles. He never returned to Cleveland, subsequently bringing his entire family to share in the delights of Southern California.

* * *

The first Jew had arrived in Los Angeles in 1841 as part of an overland group of pioneers to California, according to Max Vorspan's and Lloyd Gartner's "History of the Jews of Los Angeles." When Los Angeles was incorporated as a city in 1850, a census of Los Angeles County showed eight recognizable Jewish names. By the turn of the century, their number had grown to 2,500.

During the next three decades, from 1900 to 1930, word of Los Angeles' climate began its magnetic draw on Jews in the eastern United States. Consumptives and other health-seekers fled the cold eastern seaboard for the magic of Southern California, established themselves in Los Angeles, and then sent for their families. By 1930, the Jewish population in Los Angeles exceeded 65,000.

In a master understatement, the February 2, 1905, issue of the B'nai B'rith Messenger, the pioneer Los Angeles Jewish newspaper, wrote: "...the south (of California) is preferable to all other parts of the globe." Little did the early settlers from New York City, Philadelphia, Chicago and other eastern cities realize that Los Angeles would one day become the second largest center of Jewish population in the United States.

The resettlement of Jewish immigrants from New York was pushed by that city's Industrial Removal Office -- essentially

German Jews who sought to relocate eastern European Jews away from New York City, and was pulled to Los Angeles by the pioneer Hamburger's department Store, which offered transportation money for tailors.

As word of the golden climate spread, the exciting news reached into the cold Midwest as well as to the east, and a migration began from the Jewish neighborhoods of Chicago and Cleveland.

The Jews of the California "gold rush" of the 1920s were markedly different from the migrants who came 20 years earlier for their health. The new migrants came looking for opportunity and sunshine, and many had resources – some had money, most had skills.

* * *

My father came with limited money but with strong skills.

Stepping out of the gloom of Los Angeles' Central Station after the long train ride from Cleveland, he was stunned by what he found. His wildest imagination had not prepared him for the bright and warming Los Angeles morning. Only days earlier, he had left Cleveland deep in snow and bitter with cold. But here in Los Angeles it was like summer, except that the air was dry rather than humid and was bright and fresh rather than filled with soot.

The buildings were white and the streets were clean. It was like nothing he had experienced in his 29 years. The sunshine and the palm trees of Los Angeles were as far removed from the cold and the smokestacks of Cleveland as Cleveland was removed from the mud and the poverty of his Latvian birthplace.

In Los Angeles, he first found a room for rent adjacent to downtown in the Jewish neighborhood which had formed along Temple Street. There he heard about the growing Jewish section called Boyle Heights, directly east of downtown across a bridge spanning the nearly dry Los Angeles River. Although there was another growing Jewish area along Central Avenue just south of downtown, he decided that Boyle Heights was the place to live and moved to a room in that colorful Los Angeles neighborhood.

As my father explored Los Angeles in 1925, he found the city to be everything the advertisements promised: beautiful, sun-filled days even during the winter; cool nights even during the summer; colorful flowers blooming year-around; tall, exotic palm trees; red-tile-roofed Spanish stucco homes; and the opportunities spawned by population and business growth.

And Boyle Heights gave him a Jewish surrounding. Brooklyn Avenue, the main thoroughfare, had become a street similar to eastern urban Jewish communities of the day: fragrant delicatessens offering thick corned beef sandwiches; grocery stores filled with various species of herring and kosher pickles in barrels protruding onto the sidewalk; butcher shops with live chickens in cages; bakeries with fresh bagels, onion rolls and breads; candy stores in which one could enjoy a phosphate; assorted dry goods stores and everywhere were Jewish people speaking Yiddish and crowding the sidewalks.

After making inquiries in the neighborhood, Jack took a yellow trolley car to downtown Los Angeles, got off at 1st Street, and began looking for a sheet metal shop in the light industrial district along San Pedro Street, four blocks east of Broadway.

While he peered through the window of a sheet metal shop which specialized in fabricating restaurant kitchen equipment – dishwashing sinks, steam tables, venting hoods, roll covers -- the owner, a Jewish man Jack later discovered was named Mr. Butow, noticed him. Mr. Butow came out the front door of the shop and asked Jack whether he was looking for a job. Jack assured him he was, told him about his experience in Cleveland, and he was hired on the spot. In a short time, he became foreman, in charge of several other sheet metal workers. In due time, Jack sent for his sisters Shirley and Bessie.

Chapter Two: From Lithuania to Los Angeles via Minneapolis

Once You See Los Angeles, You Will Always Return

My mother was lured to Los Angeles from Minneapolis in 1926. She was lured by her sister, Sonia, who had moved to Los Angeles from Minneapolis via Seattle with her husband, Mike, who had taken a job in Long Beach with a shipbuilding company. Wanting a business of his own, Mike moved his family, including my mother's two little nieces and a nephew, to Boyle Heights. There he became a fruit and vegetable peddler – selling produce door-to-door.

Born Rivka Kolochinsky in 1900 in the Grodna section of Lithuania, my mother was the youngest of a family which fared better than most. Her father Moshe Aaron was a structural engineer, but his early death in an industrial accident left my grandmother, Anna, a widow with three daughters, Sonia, Dinah and my mother, Rifka, and one son, Sam.

As life for Jews became increasingly difficult in Lithuania and as Sam approached the age when the Russian army would draft him into years of harsh servitude, in 1910 he set off for the freedom and opportunity offered by America. This was during the mass migration of European Jews to America in the early 1900s. Concerned with the onslaught of eastern European Jews into New York City, the established German-American Jews arranged for some immigrant ships to dock in Galveston, Texas.

Sam, leaving the cold of Lithuania, got off the ship into the unbearable heat and humidity of a Galveston summer. Not knowing anyone in America, he asked an immigration official "Where is the coldest place in the United States?" The answer he received was Duluth, Minnesota. He bought a train ticket to Duluth and had to transfer in Minneapolis. When he got off the train in Minneapolis he said to himself, "This is cold enough."

A skilled machinist, Sam found a job in a machine shop and soon sent for his widowed mother and three sisters. Arriving in Minneapolis in 1911 at the age of 11, my mother took the American name Becky, graduated from high school and completed what was then called business school – typing, shorthand and bookkeeping. On graduation, she landed a position as administrative assistant to the owner of a chain of clothing stores. In time, her two older sisters married.

Sonia, the eldest, went with her streetcar conductor husband Mike and two little daughters to seek better opportunities, first to Seattle, then to Long Beach, California, and finally to Los Angeles. And Dinah, next eldest, went with her husband to Chicago where he found work in a printing plant.

Invited by Sonia to visit with her and her family in Long Beach, a seaside city south of Los Angeles, in 1926 my mother took the train to Los Angeles. Becky became entranced with Long

Beach, sent a telegram to her employer that she was remaining in California, and – with her sister – opened a children's clothing store in Long Beach.

But when sister Sonia's husband wanted to relocate to the Jewish Boyle Heights in Los Angeles, and with my mother missing her mother in Minneapolis, the sisters closed the store and my mother returned to the cold Midwest. Not for long. Southern California had exerted its magical draw, and Becky returned the next year to her sister in Los Angeles, never again to even visit Minneapolis. Her mother and her briefly married but divorced brother Sam joined her soon after.

When sister Sonia visited the local grocery shortly after my mother joined her in Boyle Heights in late 1927, the grocer inquired how her single sister, Becky, was doing. He mentioned that there was a single young man, Jack, who came into the store periodically – perhaps an introduction was in order.

Sonia smiled approvingly and the meeting of Jack and Becky was arranged at Sonia's home.

A beautiful young lady of 27 with a slender shape, dark complexion and perfectly done hair, and used to office work, my mother had long before decided she would never marry a working man nor a man who was bald. She had met a Jewish man, Sidney Grauman, on the train to Los Angeles. Grauman was building a new theater in Hollywood and she was going to look him up and through him find a secretarial position in Hollywood.

Jack was handsome – and dashing. On arriving in Los Angeles, he had met a young man who occasionally took him along to the Metro Goldwyn Mayer motion picture studios in Culver City where they got parts as extras in films before he found a full-time job. But Jack now worked in a sheet metal shop, and at the age of 31 his hairline was already receding.

Jack immediately fell for Becky, and at a family dinner hosted by Jack's two sisters whom he had brought to Los Angeles from Cleveland, Becky found a turned-over cup at her place at the table. When she righted the cup, she discovered an engagement ring under the cup. Jack's sisters applauded with glee and Becky was too embarrassed to ask for time to consider.

And so, on March 20, 1927, in the living room of Sonia's green stucco home on South Mathews Street in Boyle Heights, Jack Brower and Becky Kolochinsky were married by a local rabbi. Jack and Becky Brower rented a courtyard-style bungalow nearby in one of the then-popular stucco-coated bungalow courts sprouting up in Los Angeles, and a new Los Angeles Jewish family was begun.

Chapter Three: A New Native Angeleno

The Great Depression Slows Growth

If not for the Great Depression, my early life as a Los Angeles Jew would have been totally different.

Everything started out great. I was born on August 28, 1928, in the Jewish-sponsored Kaspare Kohn hospital in Boyle Heights – a predecessor of Cedars of Lebanon hospital which in time became the renowned Jewish-sponsored Cedars-Sinai Medical Center. My parents named me Martin Aaron in memory of my mother's father, Moshe Aaron, and my mother called me Baby Diamond. I inherited my mother's dark complexion, grew to be tall and well built, was considered handsome with a ready smile and curly hair, and was distinguished by a lazy left eye which tended to drift to the side.

At the time of my birth, there were 65,000 Jews in Los Angeles, perhaps 35,000 of them in Boyle Heights.

My father had left his position with Butow Sheet Metal to accept the position of foreman of the sheet metal department of the highly regarded Emil Brown & Company, a large restaurant equipment firm. Emil Brown was one of Los Angeles' Jewish movers and shakers.

So fond was founder Emil Brown of my father's capabilities and personality, that my parents were invited to the millionaire's elegant opening party for his new mansion on June Street in the exclusive Hancock Park area on the near west side of Los Angeles. The elegance of the party, the magnificence of the interiors, the gourmet foods, and the attendance of Los Angeles' Jewish and non-Jewish high society, became an indelible memory which my parents recalled for years thereafter.

With a well-paying position and the security of having a fatherly boss, my parents made the big move. They left the essentially blue-collar Boyle Heights and purchased a new, rose-beige-colored stucco home with a red tile roof and a rolling front lawn on Geer Avenue in the newly emerging west-side Jewish area known as West Adams, just west of La Brea Avenue. This could have been the start of a charmed life for me, growing up on the Jewish west side.

But in 1930 the Great Depression crippled the United States. Los Angeles was one of the hardest hit cities in the nation, with unemployment at nearly 17 percent. Companies closed their doors and thousands of people were suddenly jobless. Even the giant Emil Brown & Company had to reduce its workforce to the point that my father was laid off. Out of work for the first time in his life and with no employment opportunities, there was no way to meet the mortgage payments on the house on Geer Avenue.

* * *

The Great Depression, actually touched off in 1929, did not really end until the beginning of World War II in 1941. In Los Angeles, official figures showed 723,824 unemployed in 1930 and 1,036,984 unemployed in 1940. And the Jewish population was not exempt. Jewish organizations such as the Jewish Social Service Bureau tried to be of help, but it was difficult. Grants of $27 a month were handed out to those in greatest need.

As a result of the nation-wide unrest, Los Angeles' Jewish population of 70,000 in 1930 increased to only 130,000 by 1941. The increase was spiced, however, by German and Austrian refugees from Hitler's Europe, including artists, musicians, writers and actors, attracted to Los Angeles' entertainment industry.

The majority of Jews in 1929 lived in Boyle Heights – a Jewish population of 40,000 which during the Depression years increased to only 56,000 by 1938. Most lived in rental units. Immediately northeast of Boyle Heights was the more prosperous area called City Terrace, where in 1938 the 8,000 Jewish residents there generally owned their own homes.

Smaller Jewish enclaves were found in Hollywood to the far northwest and on the west side -- central Wilshire Boulevard, Wilshire/Pico Boulevard, West Adams Boulevard and Westlake Park/Temple Street. By this time, Central Avenue, the early Jewish neighborhood near downtown, had virtually no Jews left, some dispersing father south along Vermont and Western Avenues.

Jews continued to dwell together, and were excluded by gentlemen's agreements from smaller cities adjacent to Los Angeles, such as Glendale to the north and Inglewood to the south.

Although Reform Temple B'nai B'rith moved from 9th and Hope Streets in downtown Los Angeles to a magnificent edifice on Wilshire Boulevard near Vermont Avenue in 1928, organized Jewish life languished during the depression.

* * *

With no job and no home, my parents and I moved to the Ocean Park area of Santa Monica, a section of older rental homes on the Pacific Ocean adjacent to Los Angeles. There -- with the help of my Uncle Sam, who still-single held his job in a machine shop -- my parents were able to rent a house for our family and my mother's mother, my grandmother Anna Kolochinsky.

My aunt Sonia's husband Mike, who peddled fruits and vegetables door-to-door in Boyle Heights, suggested that my father try to peddle produce in Ocean Park. People always need to eat.

My ever resourceful father used a hack saw to remove the rear half of the family car and convert it into a pickup truck. He arose at 4:00 a.m. every morning, drove 15 miles to the wholesale produce market in downtown Los Angeles where -- with brother-in-law Mike's practiced help -- he purchased the day's supplies. My father told of Mike, a large-framed, strong man with a deep voice, making an offer for produce and then physically holding the seller and telling my father to load the lug boxes into his truck.

With the truck loaded, my father returned home for breakfast. He complained that as he ate, my mother and grandmother took the best fruits and vegetables from his truck.

Peddling door-to-door was common in those years for all types of items, from produce and baked goods to brushes and encyclopedias. My father would knock on each door and call out "fruit and vegetable man."

Although people did have to eat, they did not always have money to pay for the produce. On some days my father returned home with barter – a sack of flour, a household appliance and one day a puppy, which to my sorrow my mother promptly gave away so as not to have another mouth to feed. Not that she turned away all hungry mouths in need. On many days men knocked on our door asking for something to eat. My mother always made them eggs or a sandwich and fed them on our front porch.

Our family grew in Ocean Park. In 1931 my sister Diane was born and my parents had enough money so that my mother could go for the delivery to what was now Cedars of Lebanon hospital then on Fountain Avenue near Hollywood. But two years later, when my brother Erwin came along, the Depression hit harder and my mother went for delivery to the huge, grey Los Angeles County General Hospital on the east side of Los Angeles.

At the ages of three and four, I knew nothing of economic hardships and greatly enjoyed growing up in Ocean Park, where I could play in the sand and wade in the surf. However, for some reason, probably because of my mother's super cautious nature, I never learned how to swim.

The beach area had a relatively large Jewish population and I even had a Jewish girlfriend, Rachel, when -- at the age of five -- I entered Kindergarten at Westminster Avenue elementary school in the Venice area of Los Angeles adjacent to Ocean Park. By that time my parents had rented a larger house on Second Avenue in Venice. When I was in the second grade, Rachel moved with her family to some far off place called Palestine, so I quickly acquired a new girlfriend, Margie, at school. At Westminster Avenue elementary school, I had quickly become one of the "in" guys.

Adding to the joy of the beach area were two piers, the Ocean Park Pier and the Venice Pier. Each had the exciting entertainment venues of the 1930s – rides, carnival games, and stands selling ice cream, soft drinks and french fries. The Ocean Park Pier featured a huge indoor public plunge, a dance hall and the beautiful Dome movie theater. A broad concrete walkway extended between the two piers and the pedestrians were heavily Jewish, stopping from time-to-time to chat with friends who sat on the benches spaced along the way.

Our several years at the beach were made even brighter by my teen-age cousins Yetta and Harold Furst. Yetta had a job at an upscale women's clothing store, and she would take us to the beach and buy us gifts during the year. Harold would carry me on his shoulders to movies at the Dome theater and take me for a malt afterward., showing me how to blow the paper cover off the straw.

It is necessary to note that Yetta, Harold and their brother Arthur were the children of my mother's sister Dinah who had moved to Chicago from Minneapolis after she was married . Dinah and her husband had a girl, Yetta, and two boys, Arthur and Harold.. But the children were orphaned in Chicago at the ages of 6, 4 and 2 when both parents succumbed to the national flu epidemic of 1917.

Yetta, age six, and Harold, age two, were brought to Minneapolis by my grandmother, my mother and my uncle Sam. They subsequently came to Los Angeles with my grandmother to be with my mother and aunt Sonia, and my uncle Sam followed a few years later. My grandmother, with the assistance of my mother and the financial aid of my uncle, raised Yetta and Harold in the Ocean Park and Venice beach area, and they were to me like an older sister and brother.

Arthur, the middle child, at the age of four was entrusted to my aunt Sonia and uncle Mike -- who then had two little daughters, Norma and Rose -- and they brought Arthur to California with them before the rest of the family arrived.

Occupying some of my time during those years were weekly trips with my mother on the red Pacific Electric streetcar train into downtown Los Angeles. There, in the tall Roosevelt Building on Seventh Street, was Dr. Percy Goldberg, reputedly one of Southern California's top ophthalmologists. I was born with a weak left eye – called a lazy eye – which gave me limited vision in that eye and which permitted the eye to drift to the left.

Dr. Goldberg would bandage my good right eye for a week, which I detested, to make me use the left eye. I also had a pirate's patch to wear over my good eye at other times for one hour each day to force me to read with my left eye. The vision in my left eye improved only somewhat, but I did become an excellent reader. However, the cost of weekly doctor's visits grew too great in the height of the Depression, and to my delight we stopped going..

A highlight of the depression years was the annual Christmas party for children given each December by movie star Marion

Davies. For at least two consecutive years, my mother took us to the party at the Metro Goldwyn Mayer studios in Culver City. There we were greeted by Marion Davies herself – a thrill for the adults accompanying the children – were entertained by a stage show; were given a special lunch; and then as we left we were presented with gifts. I recall a beautiful red scooter one year and roller skates another year.

Life at the beach was good to me, but everything changed drastically for our entire family when we finally got "the check."

Chapter Four: My Mother Called It Hell Sereno

Pre-War Anti-Semitism

"The check" came in the mail in 1935. We had moved to a large, red, wood-shingled house on Indiana Avenue in Venice, which my parents rented anticipating the birth of my brother George in 1935 in Santa Monica Hospital. There was even a screened porch in the back in which my cousin Harold lived. My cousin Yetta had married Frank Hyman, a six-foot, six-inch young man she met some years before when she was invited to a party in Boyle Heights. Frank's Jewish family had moved to Los Angeles from Canada via Denver and lived in the exclusive West Side of Los Angeles.

The red house had a huge back yard in which my father built a chicken coop. This allowed our family to keep a flock of chickens which dutifully laid fresh eggs every day.

When "the check" arrived, my parents joined hands and danced in a circle. "The check" resulted from a mass protest in Washington, D.C. by World War I veterans who were promised a bonus for serving in the U.S. armed forces. During the Great

Depression, any amount of money would have been most welcome.

But the check which arrived in the mail in 1937 was not for any amount of money – it was made out to my father in the amount of $350 – a fortune.

In anticipation of the check's arrival, my parents had contemplated my father's giving up his door-to–door peddling of produce in favor of opening a fruit and vegetable market. But where would this market be located?

Always yearning to be closer to the family he had brought over from Europe and then had brought to California, a family now including his parents, three sisters and two brothers, my father determined that the market should be near two of his sisters who lived across the street from one-another. Moreover, his parents – my paternal grandparents – lived there with one of the sisters and her husband. They lived in an area of Los Angeles called El Sereno, five miles northeast of downtown Los Angeles.

On the Fourth of July, 1935, my father – with the help of my uncle Sam -- packed up a borrowed truck with all of our furniture and possessions. With my father driving the truck and towing the family car loaded with the family and steered by Sam -- who could not drive -- we set off on the 20-mile trek from Venice to El Sereno.

In 1935, El Sereno was a lower middle-class community favored by downtown workers, especially policemen, firemen, other civil servants and lower-rung corporate employees. Situated around Huntington Drive and Eastern Avenue, the community was called by the Los Angeles Police Department the "white spot" in Los Angeles This meant that on a map of the city with black pins indicating where a crime had taken place, there was not a single pin in the El Sereno area.

Although the community was fewer than five miles north of heavily Jewish Boyle Heights, El Sereno was barren of Jews. Aside from my father's family, we found only three other Jewish families in the entire area – the Tashes, the Altmans and the Levys. Mr. Levy was a Jewish cowboy, complete with cowboy hat and shirt.

We rented a house on far south Eastern Avenue toward Valley Boulevard, next door to a house occupied by my father's sister Thelma Shatsky and her husband George and by my father's parents, and across the street from another sister, Shirley and her husband Sol. That far south of Huntington Drive, El Sereno was like farmland, and Mr. Levy even had a cow. My grandfather, Ben Brower, had a horse and wagon. Each day he rode out looking for scrap metal.

My mother instantly hated the place – next to her in-laws, whom she felt never liked her and were embarrassed by our presence; without Jewish neighbors; and over a mile from the nearest shopping on Huntington Drive. For most of our 12 years in El Sereno she called it Hell Sereno.

The day after we moved to El Sereno, to my delight I noticed four boys about my nearly eight-year-old age playing across the street. I ran across Eastern Avenue and said hello. One of the boys immediately asked, "What nationality are you?" I answered that I didn't know, but would check and be right back to them. I ran home and asked my mother. She, of course, understood the reason for the question and told me "You are American, 100 percent American."

Swiftly rejoining my new friends, I told them "I am American." The response was immediate: "No you're not, you're Jewish." That, I did know. "Yes, I am," I agreed. I never saw them again. The word was out even to the eight-year-olds – Jews had moved into the neighborhood.

The pre-World War II era had begun and the Nazi era had dawned in Europe. El Sereno residents – most of whom had never met a Jew – were not welcoming to us. One lady told my mother proudly, "I read Hitler's Mein Kampf the way I read the bible."

El Sereno's one saving grace was that it was only a 20-minute drive to Boyle Heights, where my parents shopped weekly. The ride and the treat of a chocolate-flavored soda for the kids and coffee for my parents and grandmother at a soda fountain were a weekly joy. And the ride home was exciting with the anticipation of the fresh baked goods and other Jewish foods riding with us in the car's trunk.

My mother's mother, my grandmother Anna, continued to live with us. She had slipped and broken her hip in Venice, walked with a cane and then a walker the rest of her life, and never learned English. Listening to my mother and grandmother speak in Yiddish gave me somewhat of a basic understanding of the European Jewish language.

Adding to our fresh food supply was an endless stream of milk and cheese. Mr. Levy, who owned Bessie the cow, made an agreement with my father. If my father fed and milked Bessie, he could keep all of her milk for our family, which now included four children. And my mother and grandmother turned a quantity of the milk into cheese, using empty sugar and flour sacks in the cheese-making process.

We had no refrigerator. Our perishables were kept in a cooler, a cabinet fabricated by my father with holes in the galvanized metal shelves and a pipe through the roof to allow cool air to enter. And we could not afford – nor did we feel we needed – a telephone.

An old-world mechanic, my father could do anything with his hands, from building sheds to giving us haircuts – and even to creating beautiful drawings with pencil on parchment-like paper. He leased an empty lot on Huntington Drive, the main thoroughfare through El Sereno, purchased lumber and nails from Edwards Brothers lumber yard, and single-handedly on that small site erected a fruit-and-vegetable stand which my mother named the Home Trade Market. The name was emblazoned in metal letters hand cut by my father and affixed to a high wooden frame above the entry. The concept was to trade at home rather than at a chain super-market or at the Grand Central Market downtown.

Huntington Drive was a divided road, with a broad median providing for four sets of railroad tracks. The inside tracks were for the express Big Red Cars of the Pacific Electric Railway, part of an extensive rail system throughout Southern California. On those inside tracks rushed the strings of attached streetcars from the fancy city of Pasadena to downtown Los Angeles, not stopping in little El Sereno.

The outside tracks served the smaller local Red Cars which went from Sierra Vista, the community directly east of us, through downtown Los Angeles, and then to the community called Watts in south Los Angeles. During our ten cent trips from El Sereno to downtown, the white people exited the streetcar on various stops downtown and black people boarded at these stops.

Our Home Trade Market was next to a Market Basket supermarket which was next to the Cowan five-and ten-cent store, and across the street from the Cameo motion picture theater..

The market was a success of sorts. As I matured I even took my turn selling the fruits and vegetables which were carefully stacked in bins made by my father. My parents advertised in the local El Sereno News and kept prices low -- the bananas at three pounds for ten cents and the potatoes at a penny a pound were big hits. Our family acquired some local fame as owners of the new market.

With my grandmother able to baby-sit my younger brothers and sisters, my mother would come into the store during the days, walking the mile-plus to the store. Our family had only one car, and my mother never learned to drive.. A single attempt ended when she backed the car, with us inside, into the kitchen of the neighbors across the street. My mother was used to walking. With no refrigeration, she shopped daily, carrying two or more bags of groceries all the way home. In time, my machinist uncle Sam made her a hefty shopping cart so sturdy that it was difficult to push.

I entered aptly named Farmdale Elementary School on Eastern Avenue in the third grade and my sister, Diane, entered

Kindergarten that year. My mother walked us to school, but when my uncle Sam bought me a bicycle, I rode it to school with my mother running after me so that she could walk it home and then deliver it back at the end of the school day – no sense taking chances on a new bicycle being stolen.

While my mother was not happy in El Sereno, my father enjoyed his business and his extended family, and we children settled down into a life somewhat in the country. Then came the big move.

Chapter Five: A Family Home at Last

World War II Brings Change

My mother wanted to move away from the relatives and looked hard for a house we could rent closer to the store on Huntington Drive. I don't know how she found our new home, whether in the El Sereno News weekly newspaper or a notice in the market or by word-of-mouth. But she found a small house on a huge lot, including an empty lot next door, for sale with nothing down and with apparently affordable monthly payments on the mortgage.

The two-bedroom, one-bath house sat at the rear of a 150-foot-deep lot covered with bearing fruit trees in the front – figs, plums, apricots, avocados and quince. There was no garage nor driveway, but a long concrete walkway leading to the house was lined with rose bushes.

The owners, who lived in a nice home on a nearby hill, were apparently tired of paying property tax on the little old house during the Great Depression. I recall a warm, older couple who were thrilled that they could provide housing for a large family.

We visited them monthly to deliver the mortgage payment, in cash, and they treated us to cake and cookies.

Our family moved into our very own home with glee. We four children shared a single bedroom using two sets of bunk beds. My parents were in the other bedroom. My grandmother, whom we called Booboo – our version of the Yiddish name for grandmother -- slept in the service porch where the laundry would be done.

For doing the laundry, my father built a laundry house as a separate building in the back yard. The laundry house included a washing machine, a wash tub and storage cabinets. The wet laundry was hung out to dry on adjacent clotheslines in the back yard. And my uncle Sam moved in with us not much later by adding a sleeping room – no bath nor direct connection to the house – attached to one side of the main house.

It was while we were living here that my brother Gary was born in a small maternity hospital somewhere in Los Angeles in 1938. With the addition of Gary, I was now one of five children.

The new house was on Gambier Street, three blocks east of Eastern Avenue, and the neighborhood was surrounded by rolling hills. Typical of Southern California, the brush-covered hills were green during the winter when they got some rain, but were brown during most of the year as they baked in the sun.

One of the best advantages of the new house was my delight in finding a boy of my own age, Ronnie Leon, living right next door. And he had a sister, Florence, who was a year older than my sister Diane. The Leons were Catholic but never appeared concerned that we were Jewish.

Ronnie showed me that we could make trails on the grassy hillsides by flattening the brush, and then we could slide down the hills on cardboard. Later, we made crude wooden sleds to ride on the slick grass.

Another advantage of the house on Gambier Street was that it was only a few blocks from Farmdale Elementary School, on the corner of Gambier Street and Eastern Avenue. But one day, that convenience changed drastically.

I was finishing the fourth grade when our teacher unloaded the news. The Los Angeles School District decided that the Farmdale Elementary School campus would become the site of a needed combination junior and senior high school for El Sereno students. At of the end of the current school year, Farmdale Elementary would be no more. We were to consult with our parents and by the following Monday we had to decide whether we would attend Sierra Park elementary school to the east or El Sereno elementary to the north.

The decision was easy for my mother. Sierra Park school was just over the hill and was in a comparatively upscale neighborhood, as upscale as one could get in a lower middle class community. On the other hand, El Sereno school was a fair distance away, across Huntington Drive which was divided by four streetcar tracks, and into a relatively depressed neighborhood.. My mother instructed Diane and me to tell our teachers we were going to Sierra Park.

Monday dawned, and our teacher asked each of us, row-by-row, about our decision. As my row was called, I heard student after student answer Sierra Park. Then came a stunning moment. Jeanette McDougall, to my mind the cutest fourth grader in the school, the lovely, blond Jeanette McDougall, answered El Sereno School. There was no question as to my answer when I was called. "El Sereno," I responded bravely.

My mother was not happy, but I was adamant. I put down my nine-year-old foot and would not be moved. Naturally, I never told her why I insisted on attending this rather miserable school.

So when the school year began in the fall of 1938, my sister walked with our neighbors east over the hill to Sierra Park, and I set off much earlier in the morning on my lonely safari to the north, over Devil's Hill, over Huntington Drive with its frightening tracks, to El Sereno school.

When I got there, to my bewilderment, I found no trace of the beautiful Jeanette McDougall. I assumed that she had decided during the summer to go to Sierra Park.

But I was stubborn and put in my two years at El Sereno school, noticing that the boys were poorly dressed – some without shoes – and avoiding as well as I could Mario de Lileo's fearful gang. Actually, I was asked to join the gang, but was quickly dismissed when I admitted that I was a Jew and that I had no idea whether my father and mother "did it" every night – whatever "did it" was.

And I don't really know where the big boys came from who harassed me on my way home from school on many days simply because they knew I was Jewish. I don't even know how they knew I was Jewish. I continued to change my path so on many days I avoided them.

But lunchtime was good. On most days I walked to my parents' Home Trade Market on Huntington Drive where my mother took me down the street to Love's 5 and 10 Cent Store.

There, at the soda fountain, during the Depression and with my parents barely making a living from the market, I dined on a tuna fish salad sandwich and a chocolate malted milk. Then my mother gave me a nickel for a candy bar at the adjacent market. The candy bars were four cents and for some reason I detested the penny change in my pocket – so I regularly threw it into the weeds as I walked back to school.

Most of the boys at El Sereno school were tough and I was a good student and a gentleman, so my teachers liked me. I found a boy friend, Richard Mason, but he moved away before the sixth grade. And I unknowingly started a false rumor about one of the cuter girls. I overheard the teacher asking her if she knew her Gettysburg Address. Not knowing about Abraham Lincoln's historic speech, I thought I had uncovered inside news, and told everyone that the girl was moving to Gettysburg.

In my estimation, my education in the fifth and sixth grades at El Sereno school was way below par, even for those days. In the sixth grade the boys outvoted the girls and the teacher allowed us to study aviation – we built model airplanes during much of the last semester. A patriotic highlight was assembling with all of the students at the flagpole each morning and singing "God Bless America."

Summer vacations seemed beautifully endless. I attribute this to three months measured against our few years. Ronnie would come to our front door and call me out loud every morning. I ran out and we played literally from morning to night. We played endless games of Monopoly, built sleds and rode them down the grass hills, wrote and with our sisters acted out plays for which we charged one cent admission.

Still vivid in our memories are the marble tracks which Ronnie and I constructed.. Ronnie's house was also set back on a large lot. It was here we took Ronnie's and my garden hoses, doubled them as they softened in the warm El Sereno sun, and kept them doubled by passing them through tin cans opened at both ends. The hoses were extended over chairs and outdoor tables so that they resembled roller coasters. On the doubled hoses, we set marbles so that the marbles cascaded along the track, through the tunnels formed by the tin cans, and typically falling at the end onto another hose and continuing their journey.

One summer, Ronnie decided that we could actually bake a cake. We bought or borrowed from his mother's kitchen cake mix, assembled the ingredients, made a chocolate frosting, and wow! We had a chocolate cake which the two of us demolished in a short time.

Our playtime was interrupted only by Ronnie and his sister's need to go to Catholic summer school, and knowing we were Jewish, they politely held off studying their lessons when my sister and I were around.

Our own Jewishness consisted of understanding that we were Jewish, having delicatessen from Boyle Heights on Friday nights, and watching our grandmother, Anna, chant aloud from her battered prayer books several times every day. My grandmother, who had an exceedingly sweet disposition and wore her grey hair in a bun, never learned to speak English and fearfully had to register every year at the U.S. post office as an alien. My uncle Sam would also bring home a Yiddish newspaper, the Forward, and my mother and grandmother discussed in Yiddish and in great detail the letters to the advice column. We also knew that there were some Jewish holidays.

For several Christmases, I insisted that we had to have a Christmas tree, and my parents gave in. My mother bought a small tree, I decorated it, and we exchanged presents. This practice was stopped when my father's brother came by with his family one holiday season and laughed aloud that we had a tree.

At the end of the summer of 1940 I entered the nearly new Woodrow Wilson Junior and Senior High School on the site of our elementary school. The new school campus consisted of the old two-story brick building on the corner of Eastern Avenue and Gambier Street which formerly housed the elementary school and a new, two-story beige-stucco building topped by a red tile roof. In addition, some classes were held in canvas tents with wooden floors, and the wood shop classes were held in the original wooden elementary school building dating back to the early part of the century.

There was also a boys' and a girls' gymnasium, and as a result of work done by the U.S. Works Project Administration (W.P.A.), we had a grand football field complete with bleachers.

Now my trip to school each day was a breeze – only three blocks down Gambier Street. But I had to make new friends. Few of my El Sereno elementary school classmates seemed to be visible on the large campus populated by students from the seventh through the twelfth grades, and the students from Sierra Park elementary, where I should have gone, were already in a clique.

Moreover, they were far better educated than I. In English class, they already knew about something called verbs, subjects and adjectives. I had to catch up.

My lack of popularity was instant. I was an outsider. And suddenly I really knew that I was Jewish. In the required seventh grade course in agriculture, work squads were selected by squad leaders, appointed by the teacher. I was the last to be chosen. The first thing our 12-year-old squad leader did was to asked pointedly, "Do we have any Jews in our squad?" Everyone looked around, and I took part in looking at everyone else. Not a peep out of me.

The same thing happened in required physical education. I was the last to be chosen for the squads and was the quietest when the inevitable question about any Jews was asked. To make matters worse, I discovered that I was a horrible athlete with really poor coordination. Perhaps this was because I was apparently born to be left-handed, but my father tried to convert me to be right-handed. As a result, I eat and write with my right hand, but my strength is in my left hand. I throw a ball poorly with my left hand and bat a ball poorly right-handed.

This inability to be athletic meant that I stood on the sidelines while my squad played other squads in basketball, football and baseball. But my squad of tough guys were excellent athletes, and we won the seventh grade championship. This meant that every person on the squad could receive a felt letter "W"– for Wilson – to sew onto a sweater. However, to qualify for receiving a letter, a student had to have at least a C academic average. No one on the squad except for me had a qualifying grade. So, come the end-of-the-year assembly, my name was the only one from my squad called to walk across the stage to receive a letter. I accepted the letter sheepishly as my squad mates glared at me.

I walked home for lunch most days, where my mother had a grand lunch prepared and I ate while listening to the radio. When I took my lunch or ate in the cafeteria, I ate alone. Even so, I furiously declined to take matzo to school during Passover, insisting on sandwiches on bread, which my mother assembled for me in our back yard. And I certainly did not stay home on the Jewish high holidays, as did my elementary school siblings.

The world changed for everyone in the United States the next year, on Sunday, December 7, 1941. My parents were shopping at the Market Basket supermarket on Huntington Drive and I waited in the car. A man working on the roof of a nearby house called to another worker, "Did you hear the news? The Japs bombed Pearl Harbor." I, of course, knew nothing of what or where Pearl Harbor was. But he sounded excited. That afternoon, Ronnie and I tossed a football back and forth making believe that it was a bomb and we decided to join the Boy Scouts, since they would be in the forefront of the war and not be sent away from the Pacific Coast. But we never did.

As a result of my uncle Sam living with us, our family always listened intently to the news during the evening, gathered in a semi-circle around the radio. Uncle Sam, who remained unmarried during those years, worked as a machinist, but he was a true renaissance man. He read broadly, loved opera and theater, and had closely watched events unfolding in Europe.

I remember Uncle Sam coming home one day and telling us with excitement that a man named Hitler had become head of Germany, and that he would be a problem for the Jews and for the world. Although Uncle Sam had escaped the Czarist Russian army by coming to America, he studied and embraced the Communist movement in the Soviet Union, so we doubted much of what he said about politics.

With the outbreak of the war, we remained glued to the radio news in the evening – following my after-school programs of "Captain Midnight," "Jack Armstrong" and "Orphan Annie."

And the entry of the United States into World War II had a most direct affect on our family.

Chapter Six: Out of the Depression

Boyle Heights – A Jew Among Jews

It has been said that the United States never did work itself out of the Great Depression, but that World War II took us out of it. The war effort industrial build-up was phenomenal, and suddenly my father was being besieged with job offers by his former sheet metal contacts. I don't know how these contacts were made, since we didn't have a telephone. It was common that if you wanted to contact someone, you drove or took public transportation to their home and knocked on the door to see if they were home.

So our Home Trade Market was closed and my father went to work – at two jobs, one during the day and one for several hours after his day shift. The market had obviously not done well, because during that period our car was once repossessed for late payment. Somehow, my parents were able to acquire another car, which was essential for my father's trips to the wholesale produce market in downtown Los Angeles.

The car was also our recreation. We all looked forward to rides, which my father derided as "measuring the streets." We all piled in, using apple boxes for auxiliary seats in the back, and just rode, typically stopping for ice cream.

But now, with my father working two sheet metal jobs, the money came pouring in. My mother even sent me to the local post office to purchase a U.S. War Bond. And my parents began planning an expansion of our little house. Even at the time when we moved in, my father promised that the small house would one day become merely the living and dining rooms of a future expansion.

My father was now home on Sundays -- the market used to be open seven days each week -- and he was restless. Although I had detested the agriculture class at school, I did learn how to plant vegetables and I decided one day to be patriotic and to plant a Victory Garden, made popular by the War effort. I staked out a plot about six feet by six feet on our adjacent vacant lot and began breaking the earth.

My father wandered over and asked what I was doing. "A Victory Garden," I answered proudly. "You call that a garden?," he asked. And suddenly we were engaged in developing a 50-foot-by-100-foot vegetable plot. The garden flourished and our family dined on fresh vegetables – carrots, beets, corn, string beans, radishes – but I was put to work weeding, watering, transplanting and harvesting every Sunday.

I was really put to work when the expansion of our house was underway. The plan, laid out by my father, was to add to the front of our two-bedroom, one-bath cottage a two-story structure with three bedrooms and a bath downstairs and a master bedroom with balcony upstairs. My father designed the addition and built it single-handedly, except for my grudging and skill-less help. He completed a lovely addition working until 10 p.m. every evening after work and every Sunday. When he did not work on the house one evening, worried neighbors came over to see what was wrong – they missed the hammering.

The exterior featured white wood siding, a brick wainscoting, and even a bay window. Ours became the nicest house on the street. I now had my own room, my sister Diane had her own room, and my brothers Erwin and George shared a room. Gary, the baby, shared the master bedroom with my parents. And we all enjoyed the new bathroom complete with a sunken tub, an element of particular delight to my father.

In 1942 , all Japanese-American residents on the West Coast were relocated away from the Coast for fear that they would conspire with the enemy in the Pacific. We had a single Japanese family in El Sereno – they grew flowers in the hills above El Sereno Park, our municipal playground. Their son Willie, was in my class at Wilson and was a popular student.

When President Franklin D. Roosevelt made his famous Declaration of War speech on Monday, December 8, 1941, we were in mechanical drafting class and our teacher allowed us to gather around a radio he brought to class to hear the speech. I looked around and saw Willie, all alone, working quietly at his drafting table. How that must have hurt him. The following year, his family was sent off to an internment camp. I recall standing, with countless others, on Huntington Drive while train after train of Pacific Electric red cars sped by loaded with Japanese-Americans. We, of course, did nothing.

My friend Ronnie was a semester behind me in school, and when he entered Wilson from Sierra Park he had made school friends. During the day at school, he hung out with those friends, and I understood this. In the evening, and on weekends, our friendship continued. Except on the Saturdays when my cousin Raymond came over.

My aunt Sonia and Uncle Mike, who had two girls – my cousins Norma and Rosie - - and who raised my orphaned cousin Arthur, had a son later in life. Their son Raymond was born in Boyle Heights only six weeks before I was born, and although we lived a distance apart, we became close cousins.

Raymond lived the Boyle Heights Jewish life that I could only imagine. He went to the very Jewish Hollenbeck Junior High School, Roosevelt High School, and was active in the Soto-Michigan Jewish Community Center. He was a member of a Jewish boys' club called the Knights, whose members wore jackets with an emblem of a knight on the shoulder, and his mother spoiled him completely.

Through the years, I looked forward anxiously to Raymond's birthday parties, at first with lots of boys who played cops and robbers and later with boys and girls who played kissing games. When I went to Raymond's big green house in Boyle Heights, we played together and went out for delicious chili sizes at a chili stand and for "mile high" ice cream cones at Curries on Brooklyn Avenue and Soto Streets in the heart of Boyle Heights.

When Raymond was nearing age 13, a bearded man came to his home once a week. I learned that this was a rabbi, a person strange to me. I later learned that he was tutoring Raymond for a bar mitzvah, and although I was completely puzzled as to what was going on, I attended the event. We entered a small orthodox synagogue, Raymond was almost immediately called to a riser where he quickly chanted something in Hebrew, then we left for a party at his house.

On a number of Saturdays, Raymond's sister Norma would drop him off at our house in El Sereno. We would go to the Saturday matinee at the Cameo theater – two features, a serial, a cartoon, newsreel and previews – all for ten cents, and then buy delicious hamburgers and potato chips for fifteen cents at the Cameo Sweet Shop next door.

At times, Raymond's mother took us to exciting new places, like the Wrigley Field baseball stadium near downtown where we saw a charity baseball game between two groups of movie stars -- the leading men versus the comedians. And once, our mutual cousin Arthur -- we called him Archie -- took us to a wondrous area called Westwood Village in West Los Angeles. I had never seen anything like it, with modern gas stations and movie theaters identified by high spires. In Westwood was the new campus of the University of California at Los Angeles. Archie took us to the chemistry laboratory where he studied, then to the Los Angeles Coliseum for a football game.

As Boyle Heights' Jewish population grew, it spread eastward on Wabash Avenue to an area called City Terrace. City Terrace was somewhat closer to El Sereno, and rather than busing junior high school students to Hollenbeck Junior High School, City Terrace students were bussed to my Wilson Junior and Senior High School.

As a junior high student, I was vaguely aware of a group of boys and girls who seemed to have Jewish names. But they came by bus, hung out together, and left by bus right after school. When they graduated from junior high school following the ninth grade, nearly all of them transferred to the heavily Jewish Roosevelt High School in Boyle Heights.

It was when I was in the eighth grade that an odd occurrence changed my entire life.

Chapter Seven: Journalism Changes Everything

Leadership Smooths Feelings

During the second semester of the eighth grade, junior high students were permitted to select their first elective course. During those years, the Los Angeles City School System had mid-year promotions, moving from the lower B8 to the upper A8, for example. Until the A8, all of the courses were assigned. But now, while five class periods were assigned, the sixth could be selected, albeit from a relatively short list of choices.

I knew that I wanted to take typing. But you had to have an alternate choice in case your first choice was filled. I looked at the alternate choices for boys with disgust: wood shop, metal shop, electrical shop, agriculture. Then a male voice behind me whispered to all students within earshot, "Whatever you do, don't choose journalism. You'll have to write an article for the school newspaper every week."

I had caught up with the others in English class and I enjoyed, even excelled, at the writing assignments. I had no idea what journalism was, except that it was a long word, but as an alternate choice I wrote down "journalism."

When the new semester dawned and we were handed our programs in an assembly hall, I found that typing class was full and that I had gotten Journalism I. The teacher in charge read a list of room assignments, then asked if she had missed any. I hesitated to raise my hand and call out "journalism ," first because everyone would obviously laugh at me for taking that class and second because it seemed obvious that journalism would be taught in the print shop. But I had to know, so I blurted out "Journalism I." Everyone turned to see who the freak was, but I was greatly comforted when the answer came "Room 242." That was one of the rooms in which English was taught.

Journalism I was taught by a Mrs. Brooks, a lovely, easy going teacher of English whose husband – we were impressed to learn – had a business selling toffee from a cart in front of the swank Paramount theater in downtown Los Angeles. Mrs. Brooks, not actually a journalism teacher, led the class from a textbook and submitted several of my articles to the student newspaper, the "Hitching Post" (our school mascot was a mule). The articles were used in the newspaper, which was distributed to the entire student body -- junior and senior high school. My grade for the semester was an A.

For the next semester, I signed up willingly for Journalism II, only to be summoned to the school office. I was handed my requested program of classes with a note on it and was asked to carry the program and note to a Miss Arthur in Room 502. As I walked to Room 502 in one of the temporary buildings which replaced the former tents, I read the note which asked "Should he take Journalism II or be on the staff?" This concerned me in that I had done exceedingly well in Journalism I, so why would there be any question regarding my qualifications to take Journalism II.?

Miss Arthur was a tall, plain-looking woman with long straight hair, a face free of any cosmetics, and with a slim, shapeless body clothed in a tweed suit with an ankle-length skirt. But she welcomed me with a warm smile and a twinkle in her eyes. She wrote something on the note, smiled, and told me to return the note to the office. As I walked back to the office, I glanced at her comments. She had written, "The staff – he's pretty good." I had no idea what in the world the staff was – it sounded somewhat negative, but the fact that she added that I was pretty good made it sound somewhat positive.

With the coming of September, I entered the ninth grade – junior high school at Wilson consisted of the seventh through the ninth grades – and found myself the only junior high student on the staff of the school newspaper which was populated by high school students. This changed my life at Wilson tremendously. I was suddenly a part of a group of students – would-be journalists – who welcomed me without questioning my Jewishness. Miss Lillian Arthur, the student newspaper advisor, was caring and nurturing, and I now had a place in which to hang out before school, during lunch, and after school.

The editor, Frank Tennant, became a special friend, admired my capabilities, and I was quickly promoted from reporter to star reporter and then to front page editor over several senior high school colleagues. However, the ongoing War curtailed the supply of newsprint and after a few semesters the "Hitching Post" had to suspend publication.

Not to be without a journalistic opportunity, Frank promoted the concept of publishing a small Student Handbook. The concept was accepted by the principal and Frank requested me as his assistant. And so we continued to work together. But when the job was finished, we returned to our studies without extra-curricular journalistic activity.

Even as students, the War occupied our thoughts, especially on the West Coast. We were engulfed in bomb drills, where we learned to duck under our desks; blackouts in the evenings, where we had to turn off all our lights; and the rationing of meats, gasoline and other materials. We learned to identify airplanes, to admire homes that had banners in the windows bearing blue stars indicating a son, daughter or spouse in the service, and to mourn for banners with gold stars meaning someone whose life was lost in battle.

My own family had no one in the service. My two eligible cousins, Arthur and Harold, were working in defense industries. The closest the War came to us was to a family who were long-time friends of my uncle Sam, the Olinicoffs of nearby Santa Monica. Sam Olinicoff had been a boy friend of my uncle Sam in Lithuania. Their warm and handsome son, Solly, who was in the U.S. Air Force, was shot down and killed.

In 1944 I developed a pain in my right side. My mother took me to a medical doctor in downtown Los Angeles who correctly diagnosed appendicitis and was ready to admit me for an appendectomy. I was 16 years old and protested loudly that I was not going to have an operation. My mother took me for a second opinion, and I much preferred the second doctor's prescription: he sent me home and suggested ice packs.

That night, my appendix burst and the pain was so bad I was ready for anything, including an operation. My parents drove me to Park View hospital near Hollywood which was utilized by the second doctor. He operated, found that the appendix had ruptured, and I was given a 50/50 chance of survival. Thanks to the advent of a new wonder drug called sulfa, I went home after 30 days in the hospital.

Visiting me daily while I was in the hospital used up all of my father's gasoline ration and he had to go to work on the streetcar. Cheering me in the hospital was a visit from my cousin Harold, who now lived in northern California, and who brought his Irish setter Kathy with him. Harold showed me the dog through a window in my room. Also cheering me was a visit from my father's brother, Uncle Marvin, who owned a grocery store and brought me a whole box of Hershey chocolate bars. My uncle Sam came by streetcar to see me daily.

My subsequent recovery kept me out of school for the remainder of that semester. A caring teacher gathered all of my textbooks and offered to tutor me at home, but I was way too shy for that and cringed when she visited me at home in bed. Thus, when I returned to school, rather than being in the high school class of Summer '46 I dropped back to the class of Winter '47. That turned out to be fortunate.

The class of Winter '47 was a small class, only 47 students after some had dropped out to enlist in the armed forces. In the first semester of the 12th grade, we were permitted to gather –

before school and during lunch – in Brinks Garden on campus and we grew close. In the second semester of the 12th grade we were permitted to gather on the front lawn, and we grew closer.

To my delight, three other members of the small class were Jewish: Celia Tash, Jerry Sherman and Martin Fox. Martin and I were college-bound, and we were both going to the University of California, Berkeley. Celia's family was one of the few other Jewish families in El Sereno. Jerry and Martin were from City Terrace, having remained at Wilson after being bused in for junior high rather than transferring to Roosevelt in Boyle Heights. They stayed because they were on the football team – Jerry, called "tank," was an outstanding lineman. Martin was an outstanding bench-warmer.

Actually, being Jewish at Wilson had become better a year earlier, due to a student from City Terrace who was one semester ahead of us and who also remained at Wilson instead of transferring. Sherman Levin, a good-looking and good-natured senior, was a star half-back on the football team, a star of the baseball team, and a star of the tennis team. An excellent student and highly popular as an athlete, he was elected president of the student body. No longer did some Jewish students have to be sheltered in classrooms during lunch so that they would not be harassed.

As a result, my senior year at Wilson went extremely well. I had an open spot on my program during the final semester and decided to sign up for the staff of the newly re-constituted student newspaper now called the "Spotlight." When I entered the newspaper classroom, Miss Arthur did a double-take and hugged me. She appointed me editor-in-chief on the spot.

As graduation approached, I signed up to try out as a graduation speaker. The openings were for the three subjects "Yesterday," "Today" and "Tomorrow." I selected "Tomorrow," wrote a speech and delivered it in competition with two outstanding students, my friend Martin and the highly popular Phil Stevens. In a sparkling moment that remains a highlight of my life, I was selected.

Our graduation in February 1947, shortly after the conclusion of World War II, was highlighted by my speech "Tomorrow, One World." It was a little too liberal for the El Sereno parents in the audience, but my parents and relatives – my uncles and aunts were invited – were thrilled.

Chapter Eight: Off to College – A Cal Man

The Great Jewish Migration Begins

My father's two sisters who lived in El Sereno at the time we first moved there soon realized that El Sereno was no place in which to raise Jewish children. So Aunt Shirley and Aunt Thelma, with their families and my father's parents, had long before moved to Boyle Heights.

It was in Boyle Heights, on Soto Street, that one of my father's brothers, Uncle Marvin and his wife aunt Rose, had a mom-and-pop grocery store. And Aunt Shirley's husband, Uncle Sol, had a kosher butcher shop father north on Soto Street near Wabash Avenue. Although Aunt Thelma and her family lived in Boyle Heights, Aunt Thelma's husband, Uncle George, had a large butcher shop together with his brothers in the newly emerging Jewish area on the west side of Los Angeles on Fairfax Avenue.

My father's younger brother, Uncle Harry, and his family were the first to make the move to the west side, to Hollywood. They were taking part in the post-World War II Jewish exodus from Boyle Heights to west Los Angeles – the upscale areas of Hollywood, Beverly-Fairfax, Wilshire-Fairfax, Pico-Fairfax,

Cheviot Hills and a new development called Beverlywood. And the more wealthy Jews were moving to the really upscale westside areas of Los Angeles called Westwood, Brentwood, the Pacific Palisades and the City of Beverly Hills..

* * *

Even when they moved from the heavily Jewish Boyle Heights, Jews continued to prefer to live together – to be near one-another, to be near Jewish delicatessens, butcher shops and bakeries, near public schools with high Jewish enrollment, and some to be near synagogues.

When World War II ended in 1945, there were 150,000 Jews in Los Angeles, about 20,000 more than when the war began in 1941. But a year later, that number had grown to 168,000; by 1948 the number was estimated at 225,000; and by 1951 the Jewish population of Los Angeles reached 330,000. It was obvious that a Jewish population surge had begun. Jewish population growth during that time was estimated at 2,000 per month. Los Angeles' general population was also exploding, and Jews were one-eighth of that population explosion – one of the greatest waves of Jewish immigration in history.

Much of the growth was attributed to the war in the Pacific. Servicemen from all over the United States were stationed in Southern California before going overseas. Once they had witnessed the Southern California weather – warm with little rain and no snow in the winter, moderate and dry in the summer with an absence of insects – many determined to return when the war was over.

In addition, Los Angeles -- even more than other parts of the nation -- was undergoing a tremendous post-war boom. Opportunities were everywhere, from new suburban tract homes and retail centers to the aircraft industry and manufacturing. The weather and the economy attracted war veterans, young people, and recent college graduates. In addition, a large number of retirees selected Los Angeles as their retirement city.

Jews came from the large Eastern cities such as New York, Pittsburgh and Philadelphia, and from the large Midwestern cities of Chicago, Cleveland and Detroit.

* * *

My father was offered an unusual opportunity by a man named Leon Goldberg, the brother of his sister Shirley's husband, Sol. Leon had a restaurant supply business on Los Angeles Street in downtown Los Angeles and he needed a steady supply of sheet metal items – sinks, steam tables, hoods, roll covers, refrigerated pie cases. Leon had an unused sheet metal shop above his store. My father could use the space and equipment rent-free, give Leon a priority on supplying his needs, and service outside restaurants and supply houses as well.

My father seized the opportunity and built a fair-sized business, Brower Sheet Metal, adding several employees. I worked there during summer vacations and my mother took care of the books at home. A highlight for me was lunchtime, when I went with my father to a downtown Jewish delicatessen and we ate up a storm.

Somehow, I could never find outside employment during the summers, although I always made a try, preferring an office environment to the shop. My only real job during high school was at Bullocks department store on Broadway at Seventh Street in downtown Los Angeles during Christmas vacation. Bullocks was a beautiful, even magical, highly upscale store and my friend Ronnie and I applied for stock-boy positions. We were hired and placed in the gift-wrapping department, in which it was our job to move gifts to be wrapped between long lines of beautiful high school girls. We loved it the first two Christmas periods, then detested it the third Christmas when the young girls had been replaced by servicemen seeking extra money for Christmas.

In February 1947 I transformed instantly from high school senior to college freshman. I graduated from Woodrow Wilson High School on a Thursday, returned to school on Friday to say goodbye and have my yearbook signed, had Saturday off, and left for the University of California, Berkeley, on Sunday morning.

Both Martin Fox, my high school friend, and I had received our acceptances from UC Berkeley – Cal as it was called. In California during those years, going to Cal was considered equal to going to Harvard, perhaps even better. I applied there because my cousin Harold had gone to Cal and was at that time a part of the University Extension. My friend Martin applied to Cal because his brother David had gone there and was now a graduate student at the university.

Leaving the small Wilson High School, a few blocks from home, and entering the giant UC Berkeley, 400 miles from home, was a big change to make over a single weekend, but I did it with ease.

In the spring of 1947, there was only one on-campus dormitory for men at UC Berkeley and the World War II servicemen -- with their new GI Bill of Rights paying the way -- were flowing into colleges all over the nation. Martin and I had pre-applied for, and received, rooms at a group of dormitories in Richmond, California, a city north of Berkeley reached by a half-hour ride on a dilapidated group of buses. The Richmond dormitories had been acquired by the University from the Kaiser Corporation, which had used them during the war to house shipyard workers.

Martin and I were driven to Berkeley by Martin's brother and took a bus to the dorm complex. Martin had a bright idea – that we should not share a room but rather each apply for different rooms. In that way, we would each have a roommate and therefore each gain a new friend. We reached the registration office, carrying our suitcases, toward evening. The woman at the desk found our registrations and asked if we wanted to room together. We looked at one another and as one answered an immediate "yes."

UC Berkeley was, as it remains, one of the nation's greatest universities. I registered as Pre-Legal, and enjoyed several outstanding courses. My one mistake was registering for Spanish II, which was permitted because I had completed high school Spanish I through IV in the 10th and 11th grades. But I was not especially good in high school Spanish and had not had any Spanish during my senior year. Entering a class in which everyone had just completed college Spanish I, I was not a contender. At the end of the semester, the instructor, a young Spaniard, said "Senior Brower, I should give you an F, but if you promise never again to take Spanish, I will give you a D." I promised.

A special achievement that first semester was Reserve Officer Training Corps (ROTC). This was required of all freshmen and sophomores at University of California campuses. The first week of classes, I was issued an army uniform and a rifle and walked out onto the field to march with the others – all of whom had just completed a semester of drill. I was nowhere, and the drill instructor could not keep the smile off his face at my awkward responses to his barked orders.

Determined not to stand out as the only foul-up, one day I went to the armory, checked out my rifle, and using my Army manual textbook I taught myself not only how to right face, left face and about face, but also how to port arms and present arms. At the end of the semester, I received first-place awards for performing both with the rifle and without the rifle.

With my high school journalism background, it was natural that I sought out the offices of the Daily Californian, the student newspaper, and joined the staff as a cub reporter. I enjoyed several writing assignments and received several bylines.

The summer of 1947 was again spent working at my father's sheet metal shop. I accompanied my father on his installations at restaurants. Working in the kitchens of some of Los Angeles' better restaurants, I saw food handling that turned my stomach – I decided never again to eat in a restaurant where I couldn't see the kitchen.

Returning to UC Berkeley in the fall of 1947 was a new experience. The Richmond dormitories were closed down, so Martin and I had ventured to Berkeley separately during the summer to find accommodations. We each applied to the University Co-Op, a cooperative student venture with several off-campus residence facilities. Although we were turned down for rooms, which were in strong demand, we were accepted for boarding -- three meals each day.

Therefore, we had to find rooms elsewhere. Martin found a room in an ancient rooming house near campus. His room had to be entered through a single-person common bathroom, so if the bathroom were in use, he had to wait to get into his room and to get out of it. I found a room in a private home with a family who rented an extra bedroom, but it was a rather long walking distance from campus. Fortunately, or unfortunately, there was an excellent donut shop on the way – three raised chocolate donuts for 25 cents and I frequently indulged.

The fall semester was a new experience as well because this is when new students typically enter campus and I received several invitations. One was from the Hillel Foundation, the organization open to Jewish students. At the one and only social I attended, I met a lovely young freshman co-ed from Canada, who invited me to accompany her to another social to which she was invited at International House. I enjoyed being with her, but I never got around to asking her out. To this point, I had never had a date with a girl and was really too shy to ask.

Another invitation came – I don't know why – from a Jewish fraternity, Pi Lambda Phi. Perhaps it was because I was on the staff of the Daily Cal. I went to the invitational dinner at the swank Claremont Hotel in the Berkeley hills. All of the guests introduced themselves, and I stood up and said "From the city that owns the golden sunshine, beautiful Los Angeles, California, I am Martin Brower." This apparently went over big, it received a laugh and a later invitation to have lunch with some of the fraternity members at a local restaurant. At the lunch, they asked me to pledge the fraternity and I agreed.

Fraternity life put me on a new social pedestal. I was able to hang out with the others on the steps of Wheeler Hall, where the Jewish fraternity and sorority people gathered. I was able to go with the gang to the football games – an exciting season for Cal because of a new, winning coach, Lynn "Pappy" Waldorf. And I had my first date. At a gathering with Jewish sorority Delta Phi Epsilon, I had met an attractive young lady from Los Angeles and asked her out. For the date, another pledge at my fraternity and I rented a car and we double-dated in San Francisco.

An aspect of living in Berkeley I also enjoyed was the travel to and from Los Angeles. No one I knew went by air in 1947. I would most frequently take the posh Southern Pacific Railroad Daylight -- which went directly along the coast from Los Angeles to San Francisco; and for a change I would periodically take a bus-and-train combo – a Continental Trailways bus from Los Angeles through the Ridge Route to Bakersfield connecting with a Union Pacific train from Bakersfield to Berkeley.

Of course, each trip home meant extra cost. And the fraternity also created extra cost – initiation fee and monthly dues. These costs, along with the cost of room and board, eventually led to my departure from UC Berkeley after only two semesters. Once again I became a full-time Los Angeles Jew.

Chapter Nine: A Return to Los Angeles and UCLA

The Fabulous Jewish Westside

In the summer of 1947, as a college freshman, I discovered that our family was relatively poor. During that summer vacation from UC Berkeley, my mother suggested -- somewhat tentatively because she was always gentle with me -- that perhaps I would like to transfer from UC Berkeley to UCLA. I assured her that I did not like the idea. Cal was a phenomenal place.

Then she explained to me that she and my father could not easily continue to send me a check every month. The registration fee for University of California schools in those days was nominal – something like $27 per semester. But the room and board, books and incidentals of living away from home – including transportation back and forth – did require a monthly check.

Initially, this did not deter me from returning to UC Berkeley for the fall 1947 semester. I had several hundred dollars in a savings account and I determined to pay my own way. It was when I saw how fast my savings disappeared, and that I could not really afford belonging to a fraternity, that I realized a transfer to UCLA and home was required.

And so, in February of 1948, I entered the University of California at Los Angeles – UCLA.

The UCLA campus in Westwood was strikingly different from that of Cal in Berkeley. Cal, developed over many generations, rested on the rather steep, cool Berkeley hills among mature trees. Its buildings represented a variety of architectural styles focused on the tall, inspiring Campanile bell tower. In contrast, UCLA's warm campus was nearly brand new with somewhat similar brick-covered buildings of Italian Renaissance design resting on two sides of a grass-covered and sun-kissed quadrangle.

In 1948 there were no dormitories for men on campus and only a single dormitory for women. That didn't matter to me, because my transferring to UCLA was based on my living at home.

The trip from my home in the northwest Los Angeles community of El Sereno to UCLA in the far west Los Angeles community of Westwood Village was time-consuming. I walked from Gambier Street up Eastern Avenue to Huntington Drive, which took about 15 minutes. Then I boarded the Watts/Sierra Vista streetcar to downtown Los Angeles, another 30 minutes. I got off at Fifth and Main Streets and walked four blocks to Grand Avenue where I boarded the UCLA-Wilshire bus to Westwood – a one-hour ride that did give me time to read my textbooks. Years later, when I too often told my children of this travel routine, they would complain "not that Abraham Lincoln story again."

In 1948, UCLA had a Jewish population estimated at near 20 percent. While gentile fraternity and sorority students gathered on the steps of Royce Hall, Jewish fraternity and sorority students gathered across the quadrangle on the Library steps. But I made no attempt to contact the UCLA chapter of Pi Lambda Phi or any other fraternity – nor was I asked to join. Instead, I went to the offices of the UCLA Daily Bruin and signed up as a reporter – a move which dominated my life at UCLA through graduation.

On a few days, my father gave me his car to drive to UCLA. On those days, he took the streetcar to his downtown Los Angeles sheet metal shop, and sometimes I would pick him up on a designated corner at a designated time to take him home. When I did not arrange to pick him up, and he took the streetcar home, I would drive home through Hollywood, frequently stopping at the NBC and CBS radio studios on Sunset Boulevard to wait in line to witness live radio broadcasts.

In love with radio, and dreaming of myself as a radio announcer, I would periodically write for tickets to major national radio programs which had live studio audiences, requesting a certain day and spacing the shows so I could go from one to another. I requested two tickets and took my sister, Diane, with me. It was a special thrill to sit in the studio and watch such live radio shows as Lux Radio Theater, the Red Skelton Show and Jack Benny being broadcast from coast-to-coast.

On transferring from Cal to UCLA, I found I had taken courses at Cal not required by UCLA and that I needed courses at UCLA not required by Cal. At Cal I was in the College of Letters and Science as a Pre-Legal major. To transfer without too much time lost, at UCLA I had to enroll in what was then the undergraduate School of Business Administration. Looking at the several fields of concentration offered within the business major, I selected Marketing.

Knowing the problems I encountered in Woodrow Wilson High School as a Jew, and noting that my sister Diane was beginning to have a difficult time forming friendships and that my once-popular brother Erwin was suddenly not being invited to parties for the same reason, my mother began dreaming of moving from El Sereno to the Jewish westside of Los Angeles. She scoured the newspaper classified ads to find a house that would be affordable – but most of the homes on the westside were in the over-$10,000 range, not really affordable even with the sale of our expanded El Sereno house.

I, too, studied the classified ads and one day discovered an ad for a house that I understood to be within our means – under $10,000. The house was on High Point Street, near the intersection of Pico Boulevard and Fairfax Avenue – a completely Jewish area -- and it was priced at $9,500.

When we went to see the two-story house at 1540 Hi Point Street, we immediately saw that it was quite different from the other homes around it. The other homes had Spanish red tile roofs and exterior walls of stucco – pink, rose, white, beige, even light green. But this house was faced with wood siding and the smaller asphalt-roofed second story seemed to be plopped atop the first like an afterthought. Moreover, the foundation was sinking at one side. Inside, the floors were bare and there was no central heat.

But we loved it. The neighborhood was beautiful and while it was certainly only middle-class for its time, to us it was upper class. Broad lawns in front of the homes were well maintained by Japanese gardeners working under the sunshine wearing their ever-present white pith helmets. My brother, Erwin, 15 years old at the time and always clothes-conscious, enthused that one couldn't wear blue jeans in this neighborhood – one would have to wear "suit pants."

Somehow, my parents came up with the down payment, which I assume was lent to them by my Uncle Sam pending sale of the El Sereno house, which was sold shortly afterward for an acceptable sum.

And so, in the summer of 1949, the Brower family hit what we considered the big time for Los Angeles Jews – we were finally residents of the Jewish westside of Los Angeles.

* * *

In 1949 through the 1950s and into the 1960s, Jewish life and shops lined Pico Boulevard from La Brea Boulevard on the east to Robertson Boulevard and beyond on the west. And to the north, along Fairfax Avenue from Pico Boulevard to Melrose Avenue, was the real center of Jewish life with bakeries, delicatessens – not the least of which was the fabled Cantor's which had relocated from Boyle Heights – butcher shops, Judaica shops and other stores operated by Jewish merchants. There were also Jewish-oriented supermarkets, including Big Town on Pico at La Cienega and Daylight on Robertson Boulevard south of Pico.

Around the Fairfax-Beverly Boulevard area, many Jews lived in two-story duplexes, with one family on the lower level and another family above. To live in this area was to be a Jew among Jews.

Our new house was on a street of single family homes and we were exceptionally proud of our location. We understood that Beverly Hills to the near northwest was far more upscale, but that was another level of living altogether. And a tract of new homes called Beverlywood was under construction west of Robertson and south of Pico. But those homes, while new and beautiful, were hugely overpriced – in the $20,000 range.

To add frosting to the cake, our new house was only two miles south of fabulous Wilshire Boulevard, the most fashionable and glamorous street in all of Los Angeles.

I recalled my first self-guided tour of Wilshire a year before we moved from El Sereno. Although I hazily remember driving along Wilshire as a passenger in my father's car on a long trip from El Sereno when I was younger, all I remember from that time is open fields.

But while still living in El Sereno on a day in 1948 when I had use of my father's car, I drove myself along Wilshire westward from downtown Los Angeles to the UCLA campus in Westwood. Opened to me for the first time on that memorable trip were sights I had never imagined:

I drove through Westlake Park on a curved bridge over the lake where my father had once taken me riding on a motor boat; passed the grand Bullock's Wilshire department store, which I later read in a retailing textbook was the most beautiful department store in America; admired with awe the stately Ambassador Hotel and the hat-shaped Brown Derby restaurant across the street; passed the green Wiltern Theater at Western Avenue; then thrilled to the Miracle Mile with its trendy shops; continued through the upscale office buildings and shops in Beverly Hills; passed the exclusive Los Angeles Country Club; then drove along the still open land along Wilshire where new two-story wood-frame apartments were being constructed; and finally went over the hill looking down on the towering signs of Westwood Village.

Now that we lived on the west side, the magical Wilshire Boulevard was actually within walking distance.

* * *

Going to UCLA from Hi Point Street was a snap. I took a blue bus at the corner of Pico and Fairfax that traveled west on Pico then north on Westwood Boulevard to the campus – 20 minutes.

More difficult than my transfer from Cal to UCLA was arranging for the transfer of high schools for my sister, Diane. My mother wanted Diane to attend the highly desirable Fairfax High School, the most Jewish school in the Los Angeles School District. This was actually the basis for my mother's dream of moving to the west side. However, we discovered that our new home on Hi Point Street was in the Hamilton High School District. A release from the principal of Hamilton was required for a transfer to Fairfax High.

Diane and I went to Hamilton at the southern end of Robertson Boulevard and met with the principal. I made every excuse I could think of for the reason for the transfer – my father drove to work in the direction of Fairfax High School; the bus went in that direction; someone we knew drove in that direction. The principal smiled and embarrassed me when he said, "I know we don't have the Jewish population of Fairfax now, but our Jewish student population is increasing." Then he signed the transfer. He was right, in the years that followed, Hamilton became far more Jewish.

But Fairfax High was Fairfax High. My sister immediately had a large group of close friends, and with them joined a local B'nai B'rith Girls chapter. And when my brother Erwin graduated from Louis Pasteur Junior High School, near our new home, he was able to go directly to Fairfax because his sister was there. The friends he made at Fairfax remain his friends even today.

My brothers George and Gary both went to Louis Pasteur but elected to go to Hamilton. Both had Jewish friends there, and George became immensely popular as co-captain of the basketball team and a student government leader. And UCLA actually worked out extremely well for me.

Chapter Ten: The UCLA Daily Bruin

A "Jewish" University

In 1948, the offices of the UCLA student newspaper, the Daily Bruin, were located on the second floor of the Student Union, then housed in the Gothic-style Kerckhoff Hall located down a short hill called Bruin Walk from the campus quadrangle. The tabloid-sized Daily Bruin was published Monday through Friday as an independent publication of the Associated Students of UCLA, itself independent of the University.

In the hefty first issue of the new semester was an article for which I was searching, inviting students interested in becoming a reporter to apply in person. I found the Daily Bruin offices, volunteered to join the staff as a reporter, and was immediately assigned articles that took me all over the beautiful Italian Romanesque campus. In addition, an occasional byline gave me some self-importance.

The Daily Bruin immediately provided me with a place to hang out during hours away from the classroom and in a short time gave me an assortment of like-minded acquaintances. The Editorial Board leaders were a distinguished group – older than I because many had been in the service during World War II and some were experienced journalists, having worked on newspapers before going into the service or having worked on military service news publications.

Daily Bruin parties were legendary, and I was now a part of this off-campus social scene.

Unlike at UC Berkeley, which was surrounded by old apartment houses with apartments for rent to students, UCLA was in the exclusive and expensive residential area of Westwood and adjacent to the really exclusive Bel Air. And there were no dormitories except for Hershey Hall, a small dorm for women. As a result, almost no-one lived on or near campus. In fact, UCLA was known as a "commuter campus."

With nearly all of the students living at home, Daily Bruin staff members whose parents had larger homes hosted the newspaper's riotous parties. Most of these homes were more spectacular than I had ever before seen – mansions in Beverly Hills, Bel Air, the Hollywood Hills and the Los Feliz area near Griffith Park. Parties usually involved beer, food, music, dancing, card playing, flirting and lots of conversation.

I became a dedicated member of the staff, a good writer and always dependable. To my great surprise, I was selected for the "reporter of the year" award at the end of my first year, an award presented at the year-end "30" banquet. To my joy, this award gained for me personal congratulations from a beautiful young Jewish co-ed staff member I never dreamed would ever approach me – a movie actress known professionally as Vanessa Brown.

As my years at UCLA progressed, I was promoted to desk editor, a position which assigned articles to reporters and edited their copy; and then to night editor, a highly responsible position which gave articles a final edit and a headline.

The Daily Bruin was printed on the press of the Hollywood Citizen News – just off Sunset Boulevard in Hollywood. As a result, the desk editor, night editor and sports night editor – a different group each of the five nights of production, including Sunday night for the Monday edition -- took the written copy and drove the Associated Students station wagon the half-hour to the Citizen News, departing for Hollywood daily at the 5:00 p.m. deadline. The trio remained with the production through page proofs, typically near midnight. A highlight was going out together for dinner, always to the Patsy d'Amour's pizza restaurant.

I learned that I was a popular boss. When I became night editor, the desk editors would gather around the weekly sign-up sheets to see which day I selected, then fought to sign up under my name.

The Daily Bruin had earlier gained some notoriety when a national magazine labeled UCLA the "Little Red Schoolhouse" during the Communist scare McCarthy years. Reacting to this label, in 1949 the UCLA Student Executive Council had voted against approval of two heavily experienced Daily Bruin staff members who were nominated by the newspaper staff to be editor and managing editor.

The Student Executive Council's reason for rejecting the nominees was the nominees' alleged Communist leanings. In response to the rejection, the Daily Bruin staff conducted an intensive freedom of the press petition drive, which resulted in an overwhelming vote of the student body in favor of the two candidates. As a result, the Student Executive Council reversed itself and approved the applicants, James Garst and Clancy Sigal.

Still, suspicions of the Daily Bruin continued, especially since the newspaper editorialized against the University of California's required faculty loyalty oath. The anti-Communist loyalty oath was imposed by the University's Board of Regents during the Cold War in 1949, and in the summer of 1950 it resulted in the dismissal of 31 non-signing distinguished professors. The requirement for taking the oath was dropped in October 1951 and the professors were reinstated.

As the older members of the staff graduated, it became apparent that the Daily Bruin was becoming an attractive extra-curricular activity for Jewish students, both fraternity and independent. As the staff became more Jewish, daily office activities and evening and weekend social events became even more interesting for me.

The step up the ladder after night editor was to run for a position on the Editorial Board. The Editorial Board for each semester was elected by a vote of the desk editors, night editors and existing Editorial Board at the end of the preceding semester. Candidates were nominated by others or could nominate themselves. The winning slate was then approved – typically automatically -- by the Associated Students Publications Board and then finalized by the mighty UCLA Student Executive Council.

I hoped to be one of two city editors, but the competition from excellent longer-term staff members would be tight. To my concern, and yet honor, I was nominated by a member of the Editorial Board to the position of associate editor. No one really wanted that position, which was to train the first-year reporters -- since UCLA had no journalism program -- and to handle the newspaper's administrative matters, from budget to planning parties. The position was typically handled by a co-ed. Before I knew it, I was elected to the position and so became a member of the Editorial Board. This still allowed me time to write for the newspaper.

I threw myself into the associate editor position, enjoying the training sessions and even enjoying the party planning. My biggest problem at the parties was that I was considered the chaperone who had to keep the senior men from seducing the freshman girls.

I don't recall that at this point in my life, as a junior, I had yet dated anyone at UCLA – or elsewhere aside from the one double-date at Berkeley.

By the end of my semester as associate editor, I had apparently done such a good job that the position – once unwanted – was hotly contested. I now had the nerve to let it be known that I wanted to run for co-city editor and was elected together with Irving Shimmer, who in later years became a distinguished judge of the Los Angeles Superior Court. Irv and I together decided on the news to be covered, making assignments to top reporters for the bigger stories; determined which articles would be on the front page; and I laid out all of the news pages. We had a great relationship and great fun all semester, and happily continued in those positions during the next semester.

By this time, 1950, the Daily Bruin editorial board had become entirely Jewish. This brought the scorn of political conservatives, especially those in the non-Jewish fraternities and sororities. But we explained that the Daily Bruin was open to all – the all-Jewish editorial board just happened.

How Jewish we were is a matter of interpretation. In later years, I referred to the group as "Los Angeles Jews." None of us was affiliated with any Jewish organization, and when the Jewish High Holidays came about, only Irv Shimmer -- whose father had a produce stand on Fairfax Avenue -- took off from school. The other Jews teased him for being so observant. I did not know enough about being Jewish to tease him.

The Daily Bruin was a mighty newspaper – or so we thought, and I believe we thought correctly. We covered the campus so independently that if the UCLA administration wanted official University notices published, we made them pay for it. Our income came from student fees and from advertising, with local and national ads. We had an Associated Press teletype in the office and covered important local, regional and national news. And we independently covered the meetings of the University's Board of Regents, sending reporters to Northern California for meetings there.

Now I felt enough confidence to date a girl. I went to a gathering of UCLA's Hillel, the Jewish students organization, and met several young ladies whom I dated, using my father's rather old car. I was still commuting to school on the bus. I also dated several of the Jewish girls on the newspaper staff, sometimes double-dating with Gene Frumkin, who also had no car but commuted by another bus from the then-Jewish area of Western Avenue and Beverly Boulevard adjacent to Hollywood. I had never considered dating a non-Jewish girl. Dating and marrying Jewish was a concept somehow handed down from my grandmother and my mother

In early 1951, I was looking forward to my final semester at UCLA before graduation with a bachelor of science degree from the School of Business Administration. My grades were not great, pretty much a B average. Somehow, with spending 25-or-more hours per week on the Daily Bruin, I never found time to read my textbooks. I bought new books every semester and sold them "used" at the end of the semester. I recall one of the bookstore's buyers remarking on the excellent condition of the books I turned in.

As a writer, I could write a B's worth on virtually any subject in the Blue Books which were used to write mid-term and final examinations, so I received few Cs. However, during all of my years at UCLA I received only two As – one in Elements of Advertising, mainly because the professor allowed me to teach the class about newspaper production, and one in Economics of Transportation, where I did read the textbook, sat in the front row and laughed at the professor's jokes.

At the Daily Bruin elections for the Spring 1951 staff, I ran for and was elected to the distinguished position of managing editor, the person who directed the day-to-day operations of the newspaper. The previous managing editor, Jerry Schlapik -- the dedicated, thoughtful son of a Hollywood producer – was elected editor-in-chief.

The rest of the Editorial Board included, among others, the position of social editor – the person responsible for what was called the social page, essentially news of parties, dances and events including news of sororities and fraternities.

The staff's choice was Helen Edelman, a talented, hard-working Jewish girl who had one problem – she claimed to be a member of the Communist Party. Helen had once been a music major at the University of Southern California, the private university close to downtown Los Angeles. She claimed that she found USC to be so conservative and anti-Semitic that she became a Communist and transferred to UCLA.

As was the practice each year, nominations by the Daily Bruin staff for Editorial Board positions had to be approved by the Publications Board and then by the Student Executive Council. The Publications Board -- with Gene Frumkin, the editor of the Daily Bruin -- as chairman, passed the nominations to the Student Council, which was always wary of Daily Bruin staff members but which this year laid in wait for what the Council knew was coming.

Schlapik, although he belonged to a fraternity, was disliked by the Student Executive Council majority because in earlier years he hung out with suspected liberal members of the staff. And solid fraternity and sorority opposition to Edelman was based on the cry of "We want a social page, not a socialist page." Both candidates were rejected by the Student Council, and the nomination for those positions was sent back to the Daily Bruin staff.

I had been approved as managing editor but began mobilizing the Daily Bruin staff to carry on a fight as was done several years before, in which we would circulate freedom of the press petitions on campus and present them to the Student Executive Council, thereby demanding approval of our slate of nominees. But to my chagrin, a majority of the staff asked me to meet with them and confided that they did not have full confidence in Schlapik's eventual approval and wanted me to be editor-in-chief. A group had spoken to Student Council leaders and they indicated that they would approve of my nomination.

The new semester was approaching and the staff felt leaderless. I met with Student Executive Council leaders who confided that they would never approve Schlapik but that they liked me because I was a business administration major (even though I was a Jew?). The staff met and nominated me, I accepted, and on a cool January evening in the formal Student Executive Council meeting room I was voted in as editor-in-chief of the UCLA Daily Bruin.

But the position of social editor was still vacant. As the next item on the agenda, to my complete surprise, a co-ed from outside of the staff was introduced as a candidate for social editor by someone on the Council and was immediately approved. This action was too much for me and I immediately stood up and announced my resignation.

The next night I was at the Hollywood Citizen News -- where we printed the newspaper – together with the entire staff, who with the exception of the Sports Department had also resigned en mass. At the Hollywood Citizen News we put out what I wrote in a black-rule-lined editorial was our last issue. The resignation made national news, with Hearst's conservative Los Angeles Examiner beginning its article "At a secret meeting last night in Hollywood..." Hollywood was what the Examiner considered the hotbed of Communism.

With our departure, what we referred to as a "scab" staff was assembled by Student Executive Council, and a thin, miserable newspaper was issued. Everyone on campus revolted and Student Executive Council and University administration leaders met with me and asked me to return. In exchange for my return and including the new social editor, I was given written assurance that our nominees would never again be rejected – quite a victory at the time.

And so I became in fact the editor-in-chief of the UCLA Daily Bruin, which included the chairmanship of the Publications Board, which therefore de facto made me a member of the elite Student Executive Council. I also received a personal letter from University of California president Robert Gordon Sproul inviting me to join his California Club -- an organization whose goal was to unify the statewide campuses. As a Cal Club member, I worked with another member, Betty Sullivan, daughter of television personality Ed Sullivan, and enjoyed meetings in such places as Ed Sullivan's hotel suite at the ultra-swank Beverly Hills Hotel.

I was indeed a big man on campus. In fact, I was such a big man on campus that I was given a priceless perk. On-campus parking at UCLA was madness, virtually impossible. But the president of the student body and the editor of the Daily Bruin were given parking stickers for the windshields of their cars, and each was given a personal parking space directly behind the student union, Kerckhoff Hall. The only problem was that although I had this priceless sticker, I had no car. I was still commuting daily by bus.

Chapter Eleven: Graduation and the U.S. Marine Corps

The Miracle Mile

By 1951, Brower Sheet Metal -- my father's business -- had undergone a significant change. Dubin Kitchen Equipment, a major customer, told my father of a space for rent next door to its store in a building owned by the firm. Dubin would rent the store to my father at a below-market rate because they would value his firm's being next door. So Brower Sheet Metal moved from the upstairs loft on Los Angeles Street in downtown Los Angeles to a larger, ground-floor space on Main Street a few blocks south of Slauson Avenue in south-central Los Angeles.

That space worked satisfactorily, but was too small, and a year or so later my father made another move. My parents found a large, free-standing building a few blocks away on Broadway just south of Slauson and bought the building, moving the shop to a building of its own. On the front of the building, my father erected a bold sign testifying to the fact that Brower Sheet Metal had a standing of its own within the Los Angeles community.

By this time, with my sister and brothers grown, my parents worked in the shop together -- my father the sheet metal professional with contacts all over the city and my mother the bookkeeper/office manager.

This growth of Brower Sheet Metal was made possible by the addition to the business of my brother, George. I had worked for my father during summer vacations before graduating from college and my brother Erwin followed suit as did George. But George had stopped out of UCLA, joined the National Guard which then meant six months of training followed by monthly weekend meetings, and he joined our parents in the business full time. He brought to Brower Sheet Metal his considerable skill, his innate head for business, and his completely enchanting personality.

My days of commuting to UCLA by bus ended in 1951 during the last semester of my senior year when my mother found a car for me. The husband of a lady she knew from the old days in El Sereno had lost his driver's license because of drunk driving and my mother offered to buy his green 1938 Oldsmobile for $50. Now I had a car on which to attach the parking sticker which I received as editor-in-chief of the Daily Bruin. What great days. I drove to UCLA daily and proudly pulled up into a reserved parking space right behind Kerchhoff Hall.

My 13-year-old car broke down regularly, but my father knew an out-of-work auto mechanic named Leonard who lived near my father's shop, and Leonard repaired my Oldsmobile every time my father rescued me by towing the car to Leonard's house. Traffic was far lighter in the Los Angeles of the spring of 1951, and once – when my car broke down on Sunset Boulevard right at the Beverly Hills Hotel -- I merely pushed it over to the curb and took a bus home until my father returned from work and we towed the car.

My new car also gave me status on the dating circuit. I had dated girls periodically during my years at UCLA, borrowing my father's car for the evening. My dating life improved earlier that year when my sister, Diane, gave me the telephone number of a girlfriend she met at Fairfax High School and whose friendship continued after they graduated and went on to Los Angeles City College.

My sister Diane's going to Los Angeles City College was my stupid doing, for which I have never forgiven myself. Diane was an excellent student in high school and, nearing graduation, asked me whether she should go to UCLA. I told her that girls did not need to go to a university to earn a four-year bachelors degree and that she should go to City College and get a two-year associate of arts degree. And so she did.

Adriane, the girl whose number Diane gave me with her permission, had moved with her family to Los Angeles from Cleveland during the post-World War II immigration boom. She was cute as a bug, had dark hair, a lovely smile and was really sweet. Although she was only five-feet, two-inches tall and I was six-feet, two-inches, we hit it off extremely well. Adriane lived with her family in what is now West Hollywood and worked some evenings and weekends at the beautiful May Company department store on the corner of Wilshire Boulevard and Fairfax Avenue in the Miracle Mile.

* * *

In the early 1950s, the area known as the Miracle Mile extended along Wilshire Boulevard from La Brea Avenue west to Fairfax Avenue. Along the Miracle Mile -- in addition to the bold, new office building housing the western regional headquarters of the Prudential Insurance Company and the stodgy but new building housing the relocated national headquarters of Carnation Milk Company -- there was an array of upscale shops including major branches of regional men's and women's clothing stores and two popular department stores. Crowds of shoppers thronged to the new Ohrbach's store from New York City, which offered major brands of clothing whose labels had been removed and the prices discounted, and the stately May Company with its "moderne" exterior design.

Adding additional excitement to the Miracle Mile were the large and colorful Carnation Ice Cream parlor on the ground floor of the new Carnation building; a stylish Du Par's restaurant; and a spacious and bright Van de Kamp's bakery and restaurant. Wilshire Boulevard's sidewalks along the Miracle Mile were filled with pedestrians, an oddity for automobile-conscious Los Angeles.

As the Jewish population on the west side of Los Angeles expanded, the Miracle Mile – adjacent to the completely Jewish Fairfax Avenue -- became the place for Jews to shop, to informally dine, and to see and be seen.

* * *

When I dated Adriane, we typically went to a movie in one of the plush motion picture theaters on Hollywood Boulevard or went dancing at the Hollywood Palladium on Sunset Boulevard.

I also took her to Daily Bruin staff parties, where her delightful presence gave me an even higher stature.

As editor-in-chief of the Daily Bruin, I earned $50 per month, and that gave me spending money. But the end of the year was approaching, and as editor I was to preside over the "30" banquet, the last event of the year. For that event, I really needed the well-dressed college student uniform of the time – a blue blazer and grey wool slacks. Such an outfit cost $50.

As I drove my Oldsmobile along UCLA's sorority row one day, a delivery truck backed out of a driveway and banged into my $50 car. The driver's company paid me $50 for damages, which I used to buy myself the desired outfit rather than repairing the car.

UCLA graduation in the June of 1951 took place in the Hollywood Bowl. My family all attended and I became the first person in my father's family to graduate from college. On my mother's side, two of her nephews, the orphaned Arthur and Harold, and her niece Norma had already graduated.

During my last year at UCLA, the University began a graduate school of journalism, and the new dean of the school was anxious to have an editor of the Daily Bruin enroll in the one-year program leading to a masters degree. In addition, one of my business school professors urged me to enroll in the two-year master's degree program in business administration.

I had once considered entering law school, and my cousin Harold was now chairman of the University of California Extension Division's program in Continuing Education for the Bar. He said he could get me into a law school, but I would have to be a credit to him by becoming an outstanding law student. However, I understood that a B average was required for graduate school, and I hesitated to tell anyone that my average, after spending most of my college time in the Daily Bruin offices, was only a B-minus. Besides, I was anxious to go to work and earn some money.

And the Selective Service draft hung over my head. The Korean War was on and the government gave college students a deferment through college, but I knew that once I graduated I would be drafted and would have to serve in the Army for the required two years.

So I went to work in my father's sheet metal shop and waited to be drafted. My super-handy brother George had by then left to enroll full-time at California State College, Northridge. By now, even though my father's mechanical ability had totally passed me by, I was fairly good at working the foot-actuated shear to cut the metal and the hand-powered brake for bending the metal. I could even rivet metal together, to a limited extent. My operation of the hot soldering irons left much room for improvement.

Looking for a real job, I went to UCLA's Bureau of Occupations, which insisted that an outstanding writing job was available in the fast-growing aerospace industry. The opening was at North American Aviation's facility in Downey, a blue-collar suburb of Los Angeles, and I repeatedly turned that down on several visits to the Bureau of Occupations.

Not necessarily seeking a writing job, I had taken some courses in retailing and thought department store management might be interesting. The Bureau had an opening listed at the Jewish-owned Eastern Columbia department store, located in a distinctive blue-toned, multi-story, art deco building on Broadway at Ninth Street in downtown Los Angeles.

I interviewed for the position, which was assistant to the operations manager responsible for the physical side of the store, from signs to showcases, and for personnel. Shortly after the interview, I was called that I had the job and went downtown to personnel to sign up. As I filled out the papers, the young lady asked me whether I was told how much the position paid. I answered no, but that didn't really matter. The position offered a great start. She told me it paid $35 per week. Making a quick calculation, I determined that $35 would barely cover carfare for the bus and streetcar to downtown and lunch. I hated to do so, but I turned down the generous offer.

No matter, because in August of 1951 came my draft notice commanding me to report to the U.S. Army induction offices in the Mode O Day Building in downtown Los Angeles on September 14. My parents tearfully dropped me off at the designated building at 8:00 a.m. and I went through the induction process, including the Army physical examination.

Toward the end of the day, the several hundred of us draftees were told that 20 of us would be inducted that day into the U.S. Marines rather than the Army. Not being brave nor athletic in the least, I felt sorry for those who were the type of brave, athletic men who might have to go into the more adventurous and dangerous Marine Corps. So I was amazed to hear my name called and the word "Marines" immediately intoned. My first inclination was to pass out, but the next name called – a very Jewish name – caught my attention and I saw that this man, quite heavy in build, was noticeably weaving as he tried to remain standing. I decided that if he could manage to remain standing then I could also put on a brave front and remain erect.

The hundreds of non-Marines were sent off that evening by train to the Army's Fort Ord in northern California. But the 20 of us who were identified for the Marines were handed Marine Corps literature and were told to wait. I gulped as I looked at the cover of the Marine publication – a photo showing a trainee leaping horizontally through a hole in a fence.

Finally, the 20 of us would-be Marines were given chits for a night in a local hotel with the instructions to report at 8:00 a.m. the next morning at the Marine Corps Recruiting Office on Figueroa Street. A huge Marine looked at me and said, "Hey, big guy, you are in charge. Make sure everyone is in the hotel tonight and at the Marine Corps office at 8:00 a.m. tomorrow morning." It was the first time that I was sorry I had grown to be six-feet, two-inches tall.

As we walked down Hill Street to the hotel, one after another of my charges darted off. All of them lived in Los Angeles and wanted to spend another last night at home. I found myself alone at the hotel. I gave the hotel desk clerk the 20 chits which the Marine had given to me and took the streetcar and bus home as well, to my parents' delight.

The next morning, my parents dropped me off at the Marine Corps Recruiting Office and to my relief the other 19 young men were also there. We filled out papers, were sworn into the Marines, and sent by train to the Marine Corps Recruit Depot (MCRD) in San Diego.

It turned out that the Marines were desperate for officers during the Korean War. Learning that some of the inductees had college degrees, the Corps determined that if these men would agree to go to Officers Candidate School for eight months in addition to the two-years required by the draft, the Corps would have some needed officers.

Two major milestones happened at the MCRD. First, as a "hey big guy who knows how to right-face" (due to my ROTC days), I was put in charge of a squad of men quartered in one of many steel-dome "Quonset" huts. September in San Diego was hot and we were continuously double-timed. Because I had never learned to swim, at first I was aghast that in a few weeks we would have to dive into a swimming pool with full gear and swim out. But as the hot days wore on, I could hardly wait to dive into the pool. If I drowned, I drowned.

Marine Corps boot camp was tough – we were yelled at, pushed and harassed in every way. The young volunteers would sometimes cry in bed at night, and I would go around and try to comfort my group. Doing this gave me the ability to maintain my own sanity.

The second milestone was a physical examination given by the Navy medics. At the conclusion, I was told that to be a Marine a person had to have 20/20 vision or be correctable to 20/20. My left eye was 20/400 from birth. "Someone could creep up on you from the left and you wouldn't be able to see the person," I was told. "Sign here that your reduced eyesight was not service-incurred and you will be out of here in 30 days." I signed.

Being mustered out was fun at first. We were housed in the sick bay and I heard music on a radio – I had forgotten how lovely music sounded. A group of us swabbed the halls of the sick bay every morning, then sat on the balcony in the sun and talked until it was time to go to the movies. One day an officer came onto the balcony and called my name. "Brower, I understand that you have a college degree." I answered that I did. "You don't want to swab halls, we have a better job for you." Thus I spend the rest of the days typing and filing in the radiology suite from 8 a.m. to 5 p.m. until I was mustered out.

I returned to my Draft Board with the paperwork that was given me, and through the mail came my new paperwork: Medical Discharge with a card indicating my service record in the U.S. Marine Corps – inducted September 15, 1951, discharged October 15, 1951. I kept my Marine Corps green dress uniform for the next 30 years, finally contributing it as a costume to a local theater group.

Chapter Twelve: $303 a Month for Air Pollution Control

Smog Strangles Los Angeles

With my brief Korean War service career concluded, it was time to go to work. It was October of 1951 and I determined to look for a real job right after the first of the year. So I applied for a temporary Christmas job at Bullocks Department Store in downtown Los Angeles, where I had worked as a stock boy during Christmas vacations from high school. I was hired as a sales clerk in the mens' hosiery department, a position which paid $1 per hour. As did all unmarried young people of that era, I lived at home, so the $40 per week gave me gasoline for my Oldsmobile and money for weekend dating.

Bullocks at Broadway and 7th Street was the second highest end department store in Los Angeles, second only to Bullocks Wilshire, and the downtown store was eight stories of fabulous merchandise magnificently displayed. I looked forward to each day's adventure in the store which catered to the cream of Los Angeles shoppers.

It was a UCLA friend, Ralph Jackson, who told me in November of 1951 about a classified ad in the Los Angeles Times which began "Any College Degree; Start at $303 Per Month." I was enjoying working at Bullock's during the holiday rush and was not yet looking for a permanent job. However, to put $303 per month into perspective, my fellow UCLA graduates with undergraduate degrees in 1951 began jobs at $225 per month; $250 was really good and $275 was outstanding. But $303?

The ad was for the Air Pollution Control District, County of Los Angeles whatever that was – and told about an upcoming Civil Service Examination. The Civil Service examination was given one evening after work in downtown Los Angeles. I applied – Ralph did not because he was working in the May Company out west on Wilshire – and I took the exam. I must have done well enough, because shortly thereafter I was invited to the Air Pollution Control District (APCD) for an interview.

* * *

During World War II, as population growth accelerated in Los Angeles, on some days – especially during the fall – the once-clear air dimmed noticeably during the mid-morning hours and whatever was in the air stung people's eyes. The blame was quickly placed on the new butadiene factories – producers of artificial rubber for the War effort. But when the War ended and the plants were shut down, the air pollution continued. Because the condition appeared to be a combination of man-made smoke and natural coastal fog, the combined term "smog" was coined to describe the situation.

In 1948, the County of Los Angeles Board of Supervisors established the Air Pollution Control District, with the Supervisors sitting as the APCD board. A renowned eastern expert was recruited to head the agency. The expert quickly determined that the cause of the smog was hydrogen dioxide emitted from the petroleum refineries near the coast, resigned the position and returned to the east.

A new director, Gordon Larson, was recruited, and Larson organized a group of scientists – aided by Dr. A.J. Haagen-Schmidt of the California Institute of Technology in Pasadena, who had encountered damage to leafy crops from air pollution.

The team, including meteorologists, determined that the same effect which brought Los Angeles its magnificent Mediterranean sub-tropical weather – a high pressure area just off the coast – also caused what was called a temperature inversion. This inversion meant that air over Los Angeles County cooled naturally at higher elevations as was normal, but at a certain point as it rose, the air began to become warmer. This placed a cap on effluents escaping into the air and held them close to the ground. In addition, air movement from the ocean was blocked by the inland mountains, trapping the polluted air in a natural basin.

It was determined that all sources of air pollution, from whatever source, had to be controlled at the source as much as possible. But it was also determined that the major cause of the eye-irritating smog was unsaturated hydrocarbons. The major source of the hydrocarbons was the production, storage and transportation of gasoline and the emissions from the exhausts of the rapidly growing number of automobiles in the Los Angeles basin.

The hydrocarbon finding was not welcomed by the petroleum industry, which commissioned a study to be done by the renowned

Stanford Research Institute. The study, funded by the Western Oil and Gas Association, quickly found that the hydrocarbon was not responsible. It took months of work by the APCD to refute the findings and to get the petroleum industry to accept the inevitability of controls.

* * *

It was into this situation at the APCD, of which I had no inkling, that I came for an interview in late 1951. The group of us, all young men who had scored highest in the Civil Service exam, gathered in a room at the appointed time, where we were told that the APCD needed inspectors. The County had been divided into 13 districts, and an inspector would be assigned to each district essentially for "public relations work." I had heard of the term "public relations" and decided that it had something to do with journalism. During a one-on-one interview with APCD Chief Inspector Lloyd McEwen, I was one of 10 inspectors hired that morning.

Why $303 per month for "any college degree"? The APCD had been using mechanical and chemical engineers as inspectors when, following World War II, engineers were suddenly surplus and were readily available. But the Korean conflict was now on and engineers were once again in demand by aerospace firms. As a result, there was a need for inspectors even without engineering degrees. We were to begin on January 15, 1952, and we had to have our own car for patrolling whichever of the13 districts was assigned to us. I quickly thought of my 1938 Oldsmobile, out of commission at the time while I road the bus and streetcar downtown to Bullock's, and answered, "Yes, I have a car."

As Christmas of 1951 turned into January1952, and as Bullock's continued to tell the part-time Christmas help that they were no longer needed, I anxiously awaited word of my termination. When word did not come in early January, I told the manager of the men's hosiery department that I had to leave to take a new job. She was dismayed, telling me that her assistant manager was being promoted to men's shoes and she offered me the assistant manager job. $1.10 an hour instead of the $1 I was earning – plus one percent of my sales. A good sales day during Christmas was $100, so that would have given me an additional dollar a day. I respectfully thanked her but told her I was moving on.

The Sunday before I was to begin my new job as an APCD inspector – whatever an inspector was – I went car shopping with my father to get the dependable car I told my new employer I had.

We went with my father's auto mechanic friend, Leonard, to a used car lot near Broadway and Slauson Avenue. While I looked at all of the flashy cars, Leonard went over to a stodgy, beige 1947 Chevrolet. "This is your car," Leonard assured me. I hated the color and design, but my father was paying the bill and Leonard was giving his time as a consultant. So that's the car I got.

However, as I drove home in a slight rain, with the engine humming, the windshield wipers moving and the radio playing, I felt well satisfied. Now I had a real car and a real job.

The next day I reported for work at the Air Pollution Control District with the nine other new inspectors. As we all became friends during the several weeks of training, I discovered that my degree in business stood up well next to their degrees in English, history and psychology.

The headquarters offices were in an ancient two-story wooden structure in an industrial district on Santa Fe Avenue at the far southern edge of downtown. Here we were trained in the broad concepts of air pollution control, with English major Mel Weisburd cracking to me during a coffee break, "What has all of that got to do with $303 a month?" Our training included reading the density of exhaust smoke using the Ringlemann chart.

We found that as inspectors, we would each be given a district of the County in which we were to inform industrial firms about the new State of California Rules and Regulations regarding air pollution control and to enforce these rules and regulations. The APCD was the only jurisdiction in the state doing that in 1952.

We were to enter every industrial firm within our assigned district; determine whether the firm had air pollution producing equipment; if so, determine whether the firm had proper air pollution control equipment; and if not we were to issue a citation for correction and inform the owner/operator of the Rules and Regulations. We were also to complete a card on each firm, listing its equipment and controls, if any. In addition, as we drove around our district we were to look for any visible emissions or noxious odors and if we found any, we were to enter the property and issue a citation.

Because we had to enter these firms, we were taken downtown to the County Hall of Justice and were sworn in as Los Angeles County deputy sheriffs, complete with a badge to keep secluded in our pockets.

To our delight, we were to work from our homes – driving directly every morning to our districts. We were to write a brief report on every stop and mail the reports to the office at the end of each day before going home. We came into the office only every-other-week to pick up our paychecks and to attend a meeting.

I was assigned District 7, a then fairly wide open area with light industry in the southwestern area of the County. This zone included the huge Standard Oil refinery in El Segundo, but that entity was off limits to me and was the exclusive province of our refinery experts.

At each bi-weekly meeting, Chief Inspector McEwen would complain that the daily reports mailed in by the inspectors were not clear. "A report should read like this," he would say, and then anonymously read one of my reports. After three months, McEwen called me into his office, told me that I seemed to be the only inspector who really understood what he wanted, and "promoted" me to District 13, the most highly industrialized sector of the County, including the grimy Central Manufacturing District east of downtown.

A few months after we joined the APCD, we all received several surprise pay raises. We began in January 1952 for the fabled $303 per month. But unknown to us, the APCD had felt this was not enough and had requested a salary increase for inspectors. The raise came through five months later, in June, and we moved up a step to $318. But then the next month, July, brought an across-the-board increase for all County employees, and so we moved up another step to $335 per month. Six months later, in January 1953, it was our annual anniversary, and that meant another pay raise to $355 per month. We felt that we had it made.

Chapter Thirteen: A Swinging Single on the Westside

The Role of the B'nai B'rith Messenger and "The Valley"

It was at this time in my life that I became closer friends with Ralph Jackson. Ralph was one of the several people who "hung around" the Daily Bruin offices at UCLA – not exactly on the staff, but enjoying the atmosphere. The son of Hollywood writer/director Felix Jackson, Ralph was born in Austria of Jewish parents and was sent to the United States as Hitler's presence began to threaten the Jews in the mid-1930s. Ralph's divorced mother, who had remained in Austria, sent Ralph to be with his father, who had left for Hollywood some years earlier and was making a name for himself in the motion picture business.

Ralph lived a different type of life than my other friends. While attending UCLA and for some time after, Ralph rented a small guest house behind a larger home in Los Angeles' upper-class Westwood area. The guest house came with swimming pool privileges and Ralph drove a Chevrolet convertible.

Ralph had called me during the summer when I worked for my father between my graduation from UCLA and my time in the Marine Corps, and called me again when I returned home. We became friends, going to the Santa Monica and Malibu beaches in his convertible – mainly to ogle girls -- on Saturdays, and met to play on the nine-hole, par-three Rancho Park golf course on Pico Boulevard and Motor Avenue across from the 20th Century Fox studios on Sundays. Afterwards, we would go to his place to swim in the pool and to make lunch – Ralph was an accomplished cook and had kitchen privileges in the main house.

With little extra money and with no job at the time, Ralph held off from joining me and my friend Gene Frumkin, who preceded me as editor of the Daily Bruin, when we went out on Saturday evenings. A frequent Saturday evening for Gene and me was a burlesque theater/restaurant in the Los Angeles South Bay area where we dined on barbequed ribs and french fries while watching the young ladies do their routines.

Our Saturday evening enjoyment was interrupted only on the nights I had a date. In the early 1950s, the B'nai Brith Messenger, then Los Angeles' premier weekly Jewish newspaper, carried advertisements for Jewish singles dances which were held on Sunday evenings. I would buy a paper every Friday and went to a dance nearly every Sunday. The venues varied from restaurants and night clubs to the Westside Jewish Center and the Hillel organizations at UCLA, USC and Los Angeles City College.

In a short time I began to know the other young men who stood on one side of the room at the dances and so met several boy friends. I also danced with, and asked out, several of the young ladies. Many of the young ladies came to the dance with girl friends or were dropped off by their parents. If the boy chose to do so, he could invite the young lady with whom he was dancing to take her home, stopping on the way for something to eat – frequently at a drive-in coffee shop.

I continued to be conscious of my middle-class status, and in several cases did not call the young lady again if she directed me to a palatial home in a really upper class area – such as Bel Air, Brentwood or the Pacific Palisades – which I feared was way above my way of life.

A significant breakthrough in my male and female friendships came when one of the young men I met at a dance told me about his B'nai B'rith Young Men organization sponsored by the local branch of the national B'nai Brith Men's Jewish organization. The local Young Men's group met at the B'nai B'rith clubhouse on Robertson Boulevard near Olympic Boulevard, not far from where I lived with my parents.

I joined, even became corresponding secretary, and met a number of fine young Jewish men. We met on Friday evenings, and when the president of the group once said that our sponsoring B'nai Brith chapter felt we should not meet on Fridays, there was a chorus of "why not?" The response was that Friday night should be used for going to religious services, and that brought the house down with laughter. Not really knowing what services were, I held back from any remarks.

The main purpose of the organization was to plan weekly socials with the several B'nai B'rith Young Women's organizations on the west and southwest side of Los Angeles. These socials were held in homes -- typically in a girl's parents' home – where young Jewish men and women would gather to chat, dance and enjoy refreshments. The result was a fairly extensive dating career during the ensuing months. On some occasions, I double-dated with Gene Frumkin. Once, Gene and I got really swanky and took our dates for dinner and dancing at the ultra-exclusive Biltmore Bowl at the Biltmore Hotel in downtown Los Angeles.

As several members of the B'nai B'rith Young Men became engaged to young women, the name was changed to the B'nai B'rith Young Adults so that the women could join.

On one occasion, I went – out of curiosity -- to a Young Democrats meeting which was held at the University of Southern California. Most of the members appeared to be Jewish, and one young lady, finding that I lived on the west side of Los Angeles, invited me to attend a Westside Young Democrats meeting at her home near Olympic Boulevard and Orange Grove Street.

The young lady's name was Rosalind Weiner, she was near my age, and she had an idea. The Young Democrats typically exerted a great effort during every election period to support a state assemblyman, state senator or a congressman from the area. This election season, there was an opening for the Los Angeles City Council from our area. What if we made a strong effort to have a Democrat elected – one of us?

Roz asked, since I was with the County of Los Angeles, whether I wanted to be the candidate. I responded – not wanting to be the candidate – that because I was with the County it would be inappropriate for me to run for public office. Knowing that she would be flattered, I asked, "How about you, Roz?"

When Rosalind Weiner came to the door of our house a few weeks later, my mother and I were among the first to sign her petition to be a candidate for City Council. Our group did put in the required effort, and in 1953 in her early 20s, Roz was elected to the Los Angeles City Council – the first Jewish Los Angeles City Councilperson in the past 50 years.

An interesting date during this period occurred when a young Jewish co-ed I knew on the Daily Bruin called me out of the blue and asked me if I would take her to the UCLA Senior Prom. Although I had graduated, she was still at UCLA, a senior, and needed a date for the Prom. I agreed, even though I knew that she lived in the San Fernando Valley – girls in the San Fernando Valley were considered geographically undesirable – and the Prom was at the Beverly Wilshire Hotel in Beverly Hills. Lots of driving.

But UCLA co-ed Betty Sullivan had coaxed her father, TV host Ed Sullivan, to be master of ceremonies, and she had coaxed actress Elizabeth Taylor to accompany a date selected by a camps-wide vote from a group of student nominees. It did sound like fun. So I drove to the Valley.

* * *

Even as the more established Jewish families moved to the west side of Los Angeles, young Jewish couples -- looking for affordable post-War housing -- moved to areas where new housing was available, typically with little or no down payment. Many young couples who met and married in Boyle Heights moved to new housing east of Boyle Heights into a formerly non-Jewish city called Montebello. And some Jewish couples found affordable housing in the non-Jewish San Gabriel Valley in the eastern part of Los Angeles County, especially in the city of West Covina.

But by far the largest segment of the young married Jewish population moved to the fast-growing, once agricultural area of Los Angeles on the northern side of the Santa Monica Mountains called the San Fernando Valley. Although there had earlier been some Jews who moved for their health to the far eastern part of the Valley to the foothill communities of Sunland and Tujunga, the move to the real San Fernando Valley began right after World War II.

The first Jewish residents crossed through the mountains from Hollywood via Cahuenga Boulevard and Laurel Canyon into a Los Angeles community aptly called North Hollywood. As word spread, more Jewish families moved westward through the Valley into the Los Angeles communities of Studio City, Van Nuys, Sherman Oaks, Canoga Park and Reseda. Other passes through the mountains such as Coldwater Canyon, Benedict Canyon and Beverly Glen also provided access. In time, driving time into the Valley was greatly improved with the completion of the Hollywood Freeway.

* * *

Several of my fellow Air Pollution Control District inspectors turned out to be Jewish, and one of them, Robert Schwartz, invited me to a social group to which he belonged. His group was called the "Tip Toppers" and were Jewish singles where the men had to be six-feet or more tall and the women had to be five-feet-eight-inches or more. Bob Schwartz lived in the fairly Jewish Rodeo Drive area in southwest Los Angeles, near the new Broadway Department Store shopping center on Crenshaw

Boulevard – one of the first suburban shopping centers in the city – just west of Liemert Park.

Although I went only occasionally to gatherings of the Tip Toppers after joining the B'nai B'rith group, I greatly enjoyed a New Years 1953 holiday with the Tip Toppers at Lake Arrowhead in the mountains near Los Angeles. We drove up into the snow and huddled in a large cabin, drank beer and coffee, and talked. This was a sharp contrast to the weekend before, when I had gone with some of the B'nai B'rith group to Palm Springs where we laid around the swimming pool in the sunshine. Just two of the extremes offered by Southern California.

But I had not given up on purchasing a B'nai B'rith Messenger newspaper every Friday and finding Sunday evening Jewish dances. One of the dances that especially caught my eye was an affair to be held at Ciro's on the Sunset Strip on the last Sunday in January 1953. Ciro's was one of the truly glamorous Hollywood nightclubs -- which included the Mocambo and the Trocadero – along a hillside portion of Sunset Boulevard from La Cienega to Beverly Hills which was called the Sunset Strip. This was the haunt of the motion picture stars who could be seen arriving in their Cadillac convertibles. And on this Sunday evening, Ciro's would be open for a Jewish singles dance.

But during the week before that Sunday, my friend Ralph had secured a girl's telephone number which was given to him by a friend who had gotten the number from his mother, and therefore was not about to call the girl. Ralph was excellent on the telephone and he called. The girl, with the odd name of Tamar, had recently moved to Santa Monica, the beach city adjacent to Los Angeles, along with her parents who relocated from Baltimore. She had invited Ralph to come to a singles dance at a synagogue, Temple Beth Shalom in Santa Monica, on Sunday. And Ralph wanted me to come along.

I told Ralph, who had never been to a synagogue, that I had been to a synagogue only twice in my life, and that I was going to Ciro's nightclub. But Ralph was insistent to the point where I had to go. He said Tamar would have a girl for me to meet.

Chapter Fourteen: A Trip to Santa Monica

A Rabbi Moves from the East Coast to Los Angeles

On the last Sunday of January, 1953, Ralph and I drove to Temple Beth Shalom in Santa Monica in style.

A few weeks earlier, I had been called into the office of Robert Chass, the chubby and always smiling assistant director of the Air Pollution Control District. He asked me if I were interested in transferring from the Inspection Division into Public Information. I had seen the Public Information sign in the hallway of the aging headquarters building, and assumed it had something to do with real public relations.

The Public Information office consisted of two people – Paul Grimes, a former newspaper man who claimed that he had been the oldest combat infantryman in the U.S. Army during the first World War, and an assistant who had left to join the Los Angeles bureau of Time magazine. On the exterior, Grimes was a grumpy old man. Lean and with a wizened look, he had drunk himself off several newspapers and when the APCD was formed, he came in off the street and told them, in no uncertain terms, that an organization such as this would need to deal with the news media and would need public relations.

Grimes wanted to hire a newspaperman to fill the now-vacant position as his assistant, but Chass insisted he try me. He told Grimes that I had been editor of the UCLA Daily Bruin and, as an inspector, I had a full year of actual experience in the field. I agreed to see Grimes, who glowered at me and said, in his raspy voice, "I'll give you six weeks – if you don't work out you go back into the field." I agreed.

Within three weeks I was doing nearly everything by myself, permitting Grimes to sit back and read through the five Los Angeles daily newspapers -- Hearst's Los Angeles Examiner and the Chandlers' Los Angeles Times in the morning, and the independent tabloid Daily News, Hearst's Herald Express and the Chandlers' tabloid Mirror in the afternoon. Grimes never again mentioned the six-week trial. In a short time, he became my mentor and my friend.

With this new position came another salary increase. Because of my new position, I was on a new salary schedule, beginning at $410 per month. Most of my fellow graduates were still making $225 to $250. With my new-found wealth, I had traded in my boring but reliable tan-colored 1947 Chevrolet Bel Air for my dream car – a nearly new rust and cream-colored 1950 Pontiac Catalina coupe with two-toned leather seats to match the exterior and with plush, rust-colored carpeting.

Driving with Ralph in my new car to Temple Beth Shalom at 19th and California Streets in Santa Monica, we felt like kings. We found the Temple and approached a table at the ground-level entrance to the second-floor social hall where Tamar said she might be found, only to see a young lady we both immediately thought quite unattractive. Ralph, who did not relish spending money, was about to leave without investing the 50-cent admission. But we had come a long way and decided to pay the 50 cents each and go upstairs to see who might be there.

At the top of the stairs was a young lady who immediately caught my fancy. "You must be Ralph and you must be Marty," she smiled.. "I'm Tamar." I never used the nickname Marty, but Ralph used that name and had given it to Tamar on the telephone. "Yes," I immediately volunteered.

There were a handful of young men and young women in the social hall, some dancing to recorded music. Ralph looked around and decided we should leave at once rather than waste our evening, in addition to our 50 cents. "Let's wait a few minutes," I said.

Another recorded song began and I decided to be brave. I walked over to Tamar and asked her if she would like to dance. She said yes, with a smile, and I took her in my arms. She was dressed somewhat differently from the Los Angeles girls I normally met. They wore dresses of taffeta fabric or the popular blouse with a poodle skirt and ballet slippers. Tamar wore what I assumed were more eastern clothes, mainly velvet. But I especially liked her hair, worn in a tied-back pony tail, her sparkling eyes, her warm smile and what I considered a lovely figure.

Ralph was ready to leave, but I told him that Tamar was in a sense his date, so we should at least drive her home. He agreed, and we drove her to where she was living with her parents – the

Chase Hotel in Santa Monica. I enjoyed her comment, "What a pretty car."

On our way back from Santa Monica, Ralph grunted "nothing there tonight." I offered, "That Tamar was cute." To which Ralph responded, "If you like her so much, why don't you marry her?" That was the last Sunday in January, 1953. Just over four months later, on June 7, 1953, I married Tamar Edith Soloff. I was 24 and Tamar was 21.

Tamar's mother, Eve (Chava in Europe), had wanted to move to Los Angeles ever since she and the family took a vacation trip to San Diego in the late 1930s. Eve Miller had left Lithuania as a girl of 18 on her own, arriving in New York City and living with various aunts, uncles and cousins. At the Jewish Theological Seminary, where she studied to become a religious school teacher, she met a fellow student, Mordecai Isaac Soloff, who had come to New York as a child from Russia. They married and had two children, Rav and Tamar.

Mordecai found immediate employment as a religious school principal and the family moved from city-to-city throughout the East as openings appeared. Finding a scarcity of written material for Jewish religious school students, he wrote his own syllabus which came to the attention of the Union of American Hebrew Congregations (UAHC), the association of Reform Jewish temples. At the UAHC's request, he wrote and the UAHC published a trilogy of Jewish history books entitled "When the Jewish People Was Young," "How the Jewish People Grew Up" and "How the Jewish People Lives Today." They were readily accepted and in a short time were used in every Reform and Conservative religious school in the United States and Canada.

But Mordecai was frustrated as a religious school principal in not being able to reach the parents of the students. Mentioning this to the rabbi of a congregation whose school Mordecai headed, the rabbi told him that the only way to reach the parents was to become a rabbi. So, married and with two young children and supported by the royalties from his successful books, he enrolled in Hebrew Union College in Cincinnati and was ordained as a Reform rabbi in a short three years, at the same time teaching Hebrew to his fellow students.

Mordecai was ordained during World War II, before the huge Reform and Conservative congregational building boom which followed the War. He served as rabbi for a number of smaller congregations, his demanding requirements for the congregation and the religious school often not meeting with congregational approval. As a result of constant moves, his son Rav and his daughter Tamar did not attend a single school for more than two years.

But Tamar did well in school, graduating from Forest Park High School in Baltimore when she was 16 and entering the University of Maryland. Her family had moved to Baltimore two years earlier when her father became head of education for the three large Reform temples in that city. At that time, Tamar's brother Rav had already gone on to Hebrew Union College and in time he also became a Reform rabbi.

Tamar's mother wanted her to enroll in a brand new university called Brandeis in Waltham, Massachusetts, the first Jewish-sponsored non-sectarian university in the United States. Tamar felt that would be too Jewish, but after two years at the huge University of Maryland she was ready to transfer.

She loved Brandies, and when she graduated with high honors in 1952, she learned that her mother's long-time dream of moving to California was coming true. Mordecai had accepted a position as rabbi of a fledgling three-year-old Reform congregation in a new suburban section of Los Angeles called Westchester in the far southwest area of the city. Thus, in late 1952, Tamar joined her father -- her mother remained behind to sell the Baltimore house – in moving to the Los Angeles area.

Tamar's father had come earlier in the year and wrote home how he marveled at walking in the winter sunshine along the beach in Santa Monica, a short distance from Westchester. He found a two-room apartment in the Chase Hotel on the Santa Monica oceanfront, and that's where the family located – Mordecai and Eve in one room, which also acted as the living and dining room, and Tamar in the other room, which also was the kitchen.

Obtaining Tamar's telephone number from Ralph, I called her a week after we met to ask her out. I had purchased two tickets to the musical "Oklahoma," which was playing in downtown Los Angeles in the auditorium of the Temple Baptist Church at Sixth and Olive Streets, the location for musicals, symphony and dance in the early 1950s. The tickets were for a Friday night.

"Thank you, but I don't go out on Friday nights," came her reply. Now I had been put off by girls before with one or another lame excuse – but "I don't go out on Friday night?" Friday night was a great date night. The week's work was over and the weekend loomed ahead.

I had no idea that Friday night was the night observant Jews went to religious services, and Tamar was observant (I found out in later years that this was typically unusual for a rabbi's daughter). Fortunately, after she said no, she added, "But call me again." Fat chance!

However, a week later in that February of 1953, I needed a date for a B'nai B'rith Young Adults progressive dinner. Our group had come up with the idea of having cocktails at one member's home, dinner at another home, and dessert and dancing at a third home. Being single, everyone lived at home with his parents even though we were in our mid-20s, so the homes were family homes and all in the west Los Angeles Jewish area.

At this time I had been dating several young ladies whom I had met at Sunday evening dances, plus my sister's friend Adriane, but I decided to ask Tamar. My boy friends told me that I was crazy to date a rabbi's daughter because I would have to go to services every Friday night. "What are services?" I asked.

This time, when I called for a Saturday night, Tamar answered "Yes." We enjoyed cocktails – probably sodas – at the first home, drove to the second home where we had a nice dinner, then drove to the third home. Walking to the third home, I took her hand – very daring on a first date – and somehow we both knew at that moment that this was it.

From that evening on, we dated exclusively, first on weekends and then every night of the week. This included Friday evenings, when I would drive Tamar and her mother to Westchester for services at her father's new congregation, Temple Israel of Westchester, which met in a church's social hall. On Saturday nights, we had "real dates."

I did not yet realize that Tamar did not like to see money, including mine, "wasted" in any form. I felt that real dates meant going to nice places. We saw Sonia Heine's ice skating show at the Shrine Auditorium near the USC campus; we dined at the Café de Paris on Sunset Boulevard in Hollywood; and we went to first-run motion pictures in Hollywood followed by hot fudge sundaes at the fabled C.C. Brown's on Hollywood Boulevard.

On a date we still recall with a glow, we went to the elegant Coconut Grove in the plush Ambassador Hotel on Wilshire Boulevard where we had dinner and danced to Freddie Martin and His Orchestra. With cover charge, dinner with wine, and tax and tip the cost was $19. That left me with a dollar from the $20 bill I brought. When the parking attendant couldn't start my Pontiac because of a failed battery, he gave me a push around the Ambassador lot in someone's Cadillac and I gave him the dollar.

I proposed marriage on March 7, 1953, six weeks after we met, and the following weekend we drove to Long Beach where the wife of one of my Air Pollution Control associates had a jewelry store. We purchased what we both felt was a lovely diamond ring for $100 and Tamar put it on after she polished her nails as we sat on a bench overlooking the Pacific Ocean in Santa Monica's Palisades Park.

On June 7, three months after our engagement, we were married in Reform Temple Beth Shalom in Santa Monica. It was Rabbi Lawrence Block of Beth Shalom who had asked Tamar to form the young singles group at his congregation, which is where we met.

Tamar's father married us, having asked Rabbi Block's permission to use his temple. Tamar's father's new congregation, Temple Israel of Westchester, did not yet have a building. And his first choice, Temple Isaiah -- Rabbi Albert Lewis' growing Reform congregation -- had not yet completed its large new building on Pico Boulevard near Cheviot Hills, adjacent to the 20th Century Fox studios.

Through my new father-in-law, Rabbi Soloff, Tamar and I became acquainted with most of the Reform rabbis then in the Los Angeles area – in addition to Rabbis Block of Temple Beth Shalom in Santa Monica and Lewis of Temple Isaiah in west Los Angeles, there were Rabbis Isaiah Zeldin at Temple Emanuel, Beverly Hills; Morton Bauman at Temple Beth Shalom, North Hollywood; Herschel Lyman at Temple Akiba, Culver City; Max Nussbaum at Temple Israel of Hollywood; Alfred Magnin of the giant Wilshire Boulevard Temple and Alfred Wolff, his long-time associate rabbi; and Leonard Bierman of Leo Baeck Temple, Bel Air.

My father-in-law's entire congregation was invited to our wedding and many attended. In addition, because I was my parents' oldest child and my father was the oldest child in his family, this was the first wedding in my father's family and the first big wedding in my mother's family, so all of our relatives were there. Tamar invited my sister, Diane, to be her maid of honor, and I invited my friend Gene Frumkin to be my best man.

Several of my friends from the B'nai B'rith Young Adults served as ushers.

The wedding ceremony came off well, but – unknown to Tamar and me who were busy posing for photographs after the ceremony -- the reception was somewhat of a disaster. Tamar's mother had arranged for an informal buffet and the caterer did not deliver as promised. As a result, there were only light snacks and this did not go over well with my mother.

My mother did not get along well with my father's family and had not seen them for some years. She felt that they looked down on her. The wedding of her son to the daughter of a rabbi was an opportunity to invite the family to a special occasion and she felt that the event was not what she had envisioned. She had already taken a dislike to my future mother-in-law, who was also a strong woman, feeling that she was dominating me. And she felt that Tamar's mother was blocking her from seeing the wedding gifts, which my new mother-in-law gathered and took to her apartment unopened.

Completely oblivious to the frustration building within my mother, Tamar and I left the wedding in our "go-away" clothes as the guests showered us with rice. Hungry ourselves, we drove to Lawry's restaurant on La Cienega Boulevard for dinner. We then spent our wedding night at an upscale motel near Pacific Coast Highway in Malibu, just north of Santa Monica. The next morning, we were off to our week-long honeymoon at Hoberg's in the Pines, a resort in Clear Lake, California, located for us by the travel bureau in the May Company Department Store on Wilshire.

Returning to Los Angeles from our beautiful week at Hoberg's – during which we enjoyed three gourmet meals each day, lounged at the swimming pool, danced in the evening to Sal's orchestra which frequently played our requested "April in Portugal," and took long naps – we drove to our new apartment in the City of Inglewood, adjacent to the Los Angeles suburb of Westchester.

During weekends before the wedding, Tamar and I had searched for apartments to rent in several parts of Los Angeles' Jewish westside, but found only aging units. The post-War apartment building boom was just beginning, and only in later years did we discover newer apartment complexes which we had overlooked.

Tamar's mother concentrated on having us close to Westchester, where she and Rabbi Soloff were buying a house to be near Temple Israel of Westchester. In later years, she showed that she had an uncanny sense for real estate. She found us a relatively new and spacious apartment in a small building in Inglewood for $65 per month.

And so began a new Los Angeles Jewish family.

Chapter Fifteen: Our First Child is Born in Hollywood

Before the Freeways, There Were Surface Streets

The Air Pollution Control District provided a phenomenal beginning for my career as a public relations professional and journalist. With my boss Paul Grimes' fatherly guidance (Paul came to my wedding and had placed an item about the wedding in famed Los Angeles columnist Matt Weinstock's column in the Los Angeles Daily News), I quickly absorbed and put to use Paul's street smarts and my native writing abilities. After all, I was 24 years old.

Paul showed me the rear entrances to the five Los Angeles metropolitan dailies. He introduced me to the city editors and to the top reporters. He also introduced me to the editors of several key outlying dailies such as the Pasadena Star-News and Glendale News-Press, and to some of the editors of key community weeklies.

Smog was a hot subject in early 1950s Los Angeles, and we issued an informational news release to the dailies and a more educational release to the community papers each week. Our releases were nearly always used and were given major display, frequently on the front page.

In addition, we worked with Los Angeles radio station KNX on a weekly question-and-answer program; I wrote and produced a series of public information pamphlets; I wrote a basic speech; I spoke to various organizations, such as service clubs and chambers of commerce, typically several times a week; and we answered continuous telephone calls from the news media, civic and governmental leaders, and the general public.

We also telephoned a daily smog forecast to all radio and television stations and we answered telephoned complaints from citizens, which hit high volumes on smoggy days.

Our office was still in a dilapidated two-story building in an industrial area of south Los Angeles near Huntington Park and plans were drawn for a new headquarters. But the Board of Supervisors recoiled at the concept of a new building for the Air Pollution Control District – one Supervisor calling it "a monument to smog." The APCD was supposed to clean up the air and be gone.

Not content with what was considered the slow pace of air pollution reduction, the Board of Supervisors ordered the County's chief executive officer to send Smith Griswold, retired head of the Los Angeles Police Department's motorcycle division, to study the APCD. Griswold and his staff determined that a change in management was required. Our beloved leader Gordon Larson was fired as head of APCD and Griswold was appointed to replace him.

Other departments were also affected, including our Public Information group. One of the County CEO's administrative assistants, 24-year-old Art Atkinson, was put in charge of Public Information and my boss Paul Grimes was retained but sidelined. Atkinson turned out to be a good administrator, telling us he would not interfere with public information operations but rather would get us the support we needed.

At that time, in 1955, the independent Daily News was beginning to feel the pressure of declining readership and advertisements for afternoon newspapers and folded. Atkinson hired for us, from the Daily News, a full-time graphics artist and a full-time photographer. He also hired a full-time radio/television professional. Now we were really rolling: in addition to everything else I did, I worked with the graphics artist to publish a monthly newsletter, worked with the photographer to create a slide-show, and worked with the radio/television man to write a weekly radio program for KABC radio.

We also rotated weekends on which one of us would man the telephones to issue the daily smog forecast to the media and to take calls from citizens. This was un-paid overtime but overtime which could be taken later as vacation days. Tamar and I loved those weekends – we would sit in the quiet office talking, reading and nibbling on snacks.

One of the first things Smith Griswold did as head of the APCD was to move us out of the old building in south Los Angeles and into a building on Fourth and Los Angeles Streets downtown. Not even Griswold could get us into a new or even a relatively new building – the building we occupied was an old-timer on Skid Row given up by the County Health Department. My drive to the Air Pollution Control District in downtown Los Angeles from Inglewood was a simple one on surface streets. There were as yet no freeways on the west side.

Shortly after we moved into our Inglewood apartment, and before we could furnish it with more than a bed, stove and refrigerator, we found that Tamar was pregnant. Her mother determined that we should have a house of our own. She found a lovely two-bedroom home in the Loyola Village section of Westchester, adjacent to Loyola University, a Jesuit college. The streets adjacent to Loyola were named for Jesuit colleges, and the home she found was on Holy Cross Place.

As a wedding present, Tamar's mother had offered us $3,000 with which to travel to Israel on our honeymoon or to buy a house. Israel was out of the question for me, time-wise and at that time interest-wise, so we bought the house. With the $3,000 down, our monthly payments were $52 on the first mortgage and $12 on the second. As time went on, our married friends who were still renting apartments could not understand why their rent on a small apartment unit kept going up while our monthly payments on a sunny house with a large yard remained constant.

On February 28,1954, we were preparing to go to an evening speech I was scheduled to deliver on the subject of air pollution control when Tamar told me she suddenly felt it might be time for a delivery of a different type – it was time to go to Kaiser Hospital in Hollywood. We stopped at the gathering of people waiting for me as speaker and told them that we had to go directly to the hospital.

It was a good thing we went, because a few hours later that evening, as I waited with Tamar's parents, our first child was born. In those days, the father waited in the fathers' waiting room and when Tamar was wheeled out of the delivery room she was cuddling in one arm a beautiful baby. She smiled and said, "It's a boy and he looks just like you." And he did. We named him Steven Joel.

Steven was born at Kaiser Foundation Hospital on Sunset Boulevard in Hollywood. I had joined Kaiser through the APCD. Kaiser was one of the first health maintenance organizations in the nation, had its own doctors and hospitals, and our friend Jack Gold, a private physician, thought that we were practically Communists for joining a medical plan he considered socialistic. We remained with Kaiser for 20 years and received excellent health care, having the same pediatrician – Jewish doctor John Diamond -- for all four of our children.

A few months after the arrival of Stevie, as we called him, we had a window shade repair man to the house, and he turned out to be Jewish. Interested in finding a Jewish family in Westchester, he told Tamar of another Jewish family living a few blocks away. One day, Tamar pushed the baby in the stroller to meet the other family – we had only a single car – and there she met Dottie Guritzky, who also had a new baby boy,

Dottie had a brother, Jack Freedman, who had just returned from the service. Dottie's mother was visiting Dottie from New Jersey and asked Tamar if she knew of a young lady for her son. Tamar quickly arranged for him to meet my sister, Diane. In a short time, Diane married Jack in a lovely ceremony in a Conservative congregation on Pico Boulevard. Jack and Diane moved into a new apartment complex, with other Jewish young marrieds, just off La Cienega Boulevard south of Venice Boulevard in West Los Angeles.

My mother's frustration with my marriage eased with the arrival of Steven, her first grandchild, and she became more relaxed with Diane's marriage to a fine young man, a computer programer with North American Aviation in El Segundo. Still, tensions were tight especially when my parents and Tamar's parents came into contact during our son Steven's birthday parties.

Our new son Steven was extremely good natured, slept late, and we were easily able to take him on short trips to Yosemite National Park, Lake Arrowhead and to Desert Hot Springs. These trips were especially relaxing to me because they took us away, even for a few days, from the tension of parents and in-laws.

My drive to downtown Los Angeles from Westchester took me up La Cienega Boulevard, over the Baldwin Hills to Crenshaw, then east on Olympic Boulevard. Someone suggested that I try going east on Eighth Street, but the first time I tried it I decided not to try it again, too many blind intersections. On that first try, a young lady ran a boulevard stop at an intersection and totaled my beautiful two-tone Pontiac Catalina. It was then time for my first new car. I went to automobile row on Western Avenue and bought a brand new 1955 Chevrolet Bel Air – turquoise and white. Tamar and I were now parents of a handsome son and owners of a home and a brand new car.

Chapter Sixteen: On Becoming a Managing Editor

Post-War Expansion Brings New Job Opportunities

Los Angeles' post-War economic expansion during the 1950s brought new jobs and increasing incomes. Moreover, the types of jobs the Jewish community held were changing in two ways. On the one hand, many of the War veterans began their own businesses, with the self-employed outnumbering those working for others. On the other hand, the younger generation, especially the Jewish college graduates, were increasingly moving into the professions – law, medicine and finance as large law firms, banks, utilities and major corporations became increasingly open to Jews. Suddenly, Jewish engineers were welcomed with open arms by the growing aerospace and electronics industries.

Southern California's huge population growth created a massive demand for new housing, and housing development became a growth industry. Jews were especially prominent in real estate development. Those with backgrounds in law and accounting, as well as others with an entrepreneurial bent, bought large parcels of land, subdivided it, and developed vast housing tracts throughout

Los Angeles County, especially in the San Fernando Valley section of Los Angeles, and in the eastern San Gabriel Valley. In the late 1950s, 20 percent of Los Angeles homebuilders were Jewish – but the Jewish builders produced nearly 50 percent of the housing.

In addition, half of the area's shopping center developers were Jewish, possibly because of their backgrounds in retailing. Jews were also deeply involved in owning supermarkets, retail shops, and – as Los Angeles became second only to New York in manufacture of clothing -- as in New York the Los Angeles clothing industry was nearly completely in the hands of Jews.

* * *

Although I was doing well at the Air Pollution Control District, with my salary up to $525 a month, I was less than happy with the new administration and with my mentor Paul Grimes being virtually put out to pasture. Secretly, in 1956, I again contacted the UCLA Bureau of Occupations and this time I was sent on an interview for a position as assistant editor of a monthly national trade magazine called Butane-Propane News.

The location was excellent -- a small, beige stucco office building on Alvarado Avenue near Third Street on the near west side of downtown, near scenic Westlake Park and swanky Wilshire Boulevard. Similar to the APCD offices and most office buildings of the day, there was no air conditioning, but the offices had large windows.

And the potential boss was extremely nice, a somewhat plump, laid back older gentleman named Carl Abel, who was editor. But the assistant editor position offered to me required travel throughout the United States 50 percent of the time. Although

I had never been east of what we then called Boulder Dam in Arizona, the concept of leaving my little family for two weeks each month was out of the question and I turned Carl down.

A few weeks later, Carl called me again. Butane-Propane News had been the property of Jay Jenkins who owned that publication and two other trade magazines he founded – Gas and Western Metals. Jenkins was selling the three magazines to giant Chilton Publications, a major publisher of trade magazines headquartered in Philadelphia. The three publications would continue to be located in Los Angeles, and Chilton was beefing up the staff. Each publication was allowed to have a managing editor. Was I interested in becoming managing editor of Butane-Propane News and traveling only as much as I desired?

I re-interviewed with Carl and with the Los Angeles-headquartered publisher of the three magazines, Frank Chapman. Chapman wondered whether I was capable of actually producing a monthly publication of 150 to 200 pages. I assured him that I was, having been editor of the UCLA Daily Bruin, and I was hired. This was May, 1956, and I was 27 years old.

When I told Art Atkisson, my boss at the APCD, that I was leaving, he was stunned. He sat down on one of the radiators along the walls of the old downtown building and asked whether I would re-consider. I told him that I had accepted the position and would leave in two weeks. He took me immediately to APCD head Smith Griswold's office and broke the news to him. I was frankly pleased with the reaction – I did not know I was so highly regarded, although I suspected that I was.

The stunning salary offered as managing editor of Butane-Propane News was $600 per month, with the promise of $650 in six months. After telling Tamar, I called my sister, Diane, to tell her the news and to confide to her – in a whisper – my new salary. She, too, was stunned by the amount.

Chilton Publications was vastly different from the County of Los Angeles. The women here were smartly dressed, with wardrobes that adhered to the seasons. The men, too, were more sophisticated. And then there was the lunch group. At the County, we brought our lunch to work in brown paper bags and ate in a lunch room. But at Chilton, if one did not have a lunch date, you could join a group that headed to a different upscale restaurant in the area every day.

The group, male and female editorial employees, always began lunch with a cocktail. If the morning had been particularly bad, or particularly good, they had two cocktails. At first I had a cup of coffee, but I soon found the cocktail to be enjoyable. A private concern was that the cost of a cocktail or two was as much as lunch, and I knew that Tamar at home hated to waste money.

Favorite restaurants in the area were Tip's on Wilshire Boulevard, the Blarney Stone on Western Avenue, the Chapman Park Hotel across from the Ambassador Hotel on Wilshire, and the Los Angeles Press Club at the Ambassador Hotel. At the Press Club, which I was honored to join, cocktails were only 50 cents each and a buffet lunch was only 75 cents. My new lunch gang was on the younger side and was not a favorite of my boss, Carl Abel, who did not join us.

When Carl and I went to lunch, it was almost always to a quiet restaurant on Sunset Boulevard which had two-course specials. We also typically began with a cocktail and frequently ended with dessert. Periodically I would duck out on my own so as to eat at Langers on Alvarado Avenue just south of Wilshire – a great Jewish delicatessen. No one else in the office was Jewish except for Jack Kay. But Jack was in advertising sales and was always out.

As I settled into life at Butane-Propane News, Tamar again became pregnant and on December 7, 1957, we had a healthy, athletic and beautiful son and named him Daniel Stuart. Stuart was for my Uncle Sam, who had passed away from a heart attack while I was at the APCD. Although Steven was dark complected like me, Danny was light complected like Tamar. And as he lay in his basinet, he thrust his arms and legs outward, already illustrating his athletic ability and his independence.

For this birth, Tamar took a little more time to deliver and after bringing her to the Kaiser hospital in Hollywood, I went to the office. Everyone in the office awaited a call from Tamar that the baby had arrived, and when the call came, everyone cheered as I ran out the door.

It was with Butane-Propane News that I took my first business trips ever. With Tamar, I flew to Seattle, Vancouver and Portland to interview natural gas and liquefied gas company officials. Then, on my own, I flew to Indianapolis and St. Louis to research articles.

A special trip was to Chicago, where the annual liquefied petroleum gas convention was held at the Chicago Hilton Hotel and the sales and editorial staffs stayed at the ultra-elegant Lake Shore Club.

Then it was on to Philadelphia to meet the president of Chilton and other editors at the headquarters then on 59th and Chestnut Streets. Joining me in Philadelphia was Don Wright, who had become managing editor of Gas, our sister Los Angeles publication. Our group publisher, who was in Philadelphia, took us to his home on the Philadelphia Main Line for cocktails and I was astounded at the beauty of the countryside. Los Angeles in the summer, with no rain, was always brown. Philadelphia was totally green.

I then continued on to a vacation in Washington, D.C., where I met Tamar, who was able to leave the two boys with her mother. I had arrived a day early and taken a room for us at the Washington Hilton. When I brought Tamar from the airport back to the hotel room, she immediately looked at the room rate on the door, saw that the tariff was $16 a day, and told me we had to find a hotel with a cheaper price.

But we remained. We visited Tamar's relatives in Washington, went on to New York City where we stayed with her Aunt Vera – who gave a massive party so that we could meet all of the New York relatives -- and continued on to Fall River, Massachusetts, to visit her uncles Abe and Ruby and their families.

Being managing editor of Butane-Propane News was exciting. I researched and wrote a number of articles each month, typically management articles, becoming somewhat expert on the liquefied petroleum gas industry. I attended conventions throughout the United States and reported on the proceedings.

And I purchased articles and photographs from freelance writers and photographers. Editor Carl Abel was the technical authority and wrote the technical articles. The "back of the book" news, personnel changes and new product information was handled by my assistant editor, Mary Lou Harrington. Mary Lou and I worked together extremely well.

I also laid out every issue. At first, we had an art department to assist on the layout, but Chilton decided that the managing editors could do this themselves, and ever since laying out the newspaper in high school and in college I always enjoyed that function.

Making the production of the perfect-bound monthly magazine especially interesting was that with the acquisition by Chilton, the publication was typeset and printed in Chilton's huge Philadelphia printshop. We mailed typed copy, photographs and dummy layout pages to Philadelphia; received galley proofs back through the mail; mailed corrected proofs to Philadelphia; received page proofs; corrected them and sent them back; and then awaited the finished magazines.

The head of printing for Chilton, a hardened veteran named Duffy, kept telling us we did better than the many publications located in Philadelphia – and he loved to come to Los Angeles to visit and to host our lunch gang to an endless string of cocktails – "Grant's scotch on the rocks, if you have it."

My parents continued to work at Brower Sheet Metal, settling into a comfortable routine. My sister Diane and her husband Jack had their first child and moved to a house in the increasingly Jewish Mar Vista area of West Los Angeles. My brother Erwin graduated from Fairfax High School, attended Los Angeles City College on the Vermont Avenue campus, and was drafted into the Army where he put his radio repair experience to work in the Signal Corps. My brother George graduated from Hamilton High School, where he was co-captain of the basketball team and an outstanding student, and entered UCLA where he pledged the Jewish Pi Lambda Phi fraternity, the same fraternity I had pledged at UC Berkeley. My brother Gary was at Hamilton High School.

In later years, I regretted being so involved with my own little family and with my career that I had no time to pay closer attention to my younger brothers as they developed into young men. I was never able to attend even one of George's high school basketball games.

Involvement with my own little family included involvement with my father-in-law's Reform congregation, Temple Israel of Westchester. Westchester, near what was then Los Angeles Airport and after expansion in 1960 became Los Angeles International Airport, was considered to be in the South Bay area of Los Angeles.

The congregation was expanding with the growth of the Westchester area and, after meeting in a series of churches and at the Westchester Women's Club, the Temple acquired a site and was building. The site was on Airport Boulevard between La Tijera Boulevard and Manchester Avenue and excitement in the congregation grew.

At the Temple, Tamar organized a Young Marrieds group and the Young Marrieds became our social friends. We met regularly, typically with a planned program, but we also all came to Friday night services and went out to a coffee shop or to someone's home afterward. In addition, we got together with various of the couples on Saturday nights. We had a fantastic babysitter a few houses away, an older lady who was always available for 50 cents an hour.

Working at Chilton Publications continued to be enjoyable, but the late 1950s were economic recession years and home appliance advertising directed at liquefied petroleum gas dealers, a big chunk of Butane-Propane News' advertising income, was tapering off. All of the Chilton trade magazines were what was called "controlled circulation." That meant that rather than attempt to attract subscribers who would pay part of the cost, the publications were mailed to every company in its industry. Thus, Butane-Propane News was mailed to every liquefied petroleum gas dealer in the United States and Canada, assuring advertisers of great penetration. But advertising carried the entire load.

With magazine income slumping, salary increases were not to be had. My original starting salary of $600 a month was never increased. My friend Ralph told me of unbelievable salaries being offered by Los Angeles' growing aerospace industry – he said that a firm called Litton Industries was looking for an internal publication editor and was supposedly offering $800 a month. He insisted that I apply, but I did not believe that a salary of $800 could be accurate.

My boss, Carl, would frequently show me his plans for retirement in a few years during our lunches. The concept was that Carl would retire and I would become editor. But everything changed when Carl, in his early 60s, succumbed to a sudden heart attack in 1959, three years after I began working for him.

A few months earlier, Carl had retained an eastern editor who was stationed in Philadelphia and who reported to me, but who had once been editorial director of Jay Jenkins publications before Jay sold to Chilton. The eastern editor was 10 years older than I and had strong experience. Shortly after Carl passed away, publisher Frank Chapman called me into his office with the good news that the eastern editor had accepted the publisher's invitation to return to Los Angeles and take over as editor.

Disappointed with this turn of events, I determined that it was time to leave the magazine.

Chapter Seventeen: At Least the Office Was Next to Pink's Hot Dogs

The Emerging World of Aerospace and Technology

Again I contacted the UCLA Bureau of Occupations and this time I was sent to an interview with a man named Norman Lynn who had a public relations agency called Lynn-Western. The office suite was in a two-story stucco building on the corner of La Brea and Melrose Avenues, much closer to the fashionable Jewish west side of Los Angeles -- and adjacent to the building was the legendary Pink's hot dog stand.

The Lynn-Western offices were air conditioned, furnished with modern desks and file cabinets, soft background music flowed from a high fidelity player, and Norm Lynn had a great smile. I would be News Bureau Director for the agency consisting of Norm, myself and two secretaries, but with great expectations.

In addition to servicing a variety of the exciting new post-War aerospace and technology clients, we would be Western U.S. editors for Steel Magazine, published in Cleveland, and for Interavia Review, a slick international aerospace magazine published in Switzerland.

Norm told me the job was mine, and that he would start me at $550 a month. I was hoping to increase my salary over the $600 I had been earning for the past three years, but told Norm that although I could not take a cut, I would start at the same salary, $600. So I called the new editor of Butane-Propane News, who was trying to sell his home in Philadelphia, and startled him by telling him that I was leaving in two weeks.

I learned a lesson in accepting the job at Lynn-Western that I have tried to pass on to everyone seeking a job ever since. The lesson is that during the time your prospective employer is checking out your background, you should be checking out your prospective employer's background. It did not take me long to discover that my predecessor at Lynn-Western had stayed on the job for six weeks before leaving. I would have liked to have left in six weeks, but I was married with two children and had to try to make a go of what was a most difficult situation.

Norm, an engineer, had inherited the public relations agency from his brother, a public relations professional, and what should have been a creative agency was run along engineering lines. And it turned out that Norm had a hidden temper.

We worked until 7:00 p.m. or later every day, trying to please clients, filing copy three times a week with Geneva for Interavia Revue and once a week with Cleveland for Steel Magazine, and never took a break. In addition, Norm had just formed an alliance with an advertising agency in the same building, and the newly formed combined firm was trying to get new business.

In the midst of this, Tamar was pregnant with our third child and we needed a larger home.

I had long wanted to move to a Jewish neighborhood and talked about looking for homes in a westside area such as Brentwood. While home prices there were high, at that time the prices were not impossible. Or perhaps the San Fernando Valley, where prices were relatively affordable. But Tamar saw no reason to leave Westchester.

With Steven ready for Kindergarten, we decided to move near Cowan Avenue School in the upscale North Kentwood section of Westchester. But homes were hard to find in 1959.

One day, someone told Tamar of a home coming up for sale on Ogelsby Avenue in North Kentwood. We alerted our real estate broker and we bought the home before it hit the market. This was a lovely two-bedroom-and-den, bath-and-one-half newer home on a slight bluff. It fit our growing family nicely.

On moving day, I took a half day off to help my pregnant wife and guide the movers. My boss, Norm, docked my pay for that half day after all of the hours of overtime I had put in every week, and I realized it was really time to leave.

Enter my old friend Ralph Jackson. During the past few years, Ralph had gotten a job as a writer on a new publication, TV Guide. He was even sent to cover the opening of a new amusement park called Disneyland in Anaheim, California. From TV Guide he joined an architectural firm called Daniel Mann Johnson and Mendenhall as the firm's public relations man. When that position ended, Ralph wandered into the most prestigious architectural firm in Los Angeles, Welton Becket and Associates, looking for a public relations position. As luck would have it, the firm was unhappy with its existing public relations director and replaced him with Ralph.

Feeling that he needed to strengthen his role, Ralph called me and asked me to become his assistant. Working for my friend Ralph was not my idea of a promotion, but it was certainly a way out of Lynn-Western. I told Norm I had a dental appointment and met with Ralph and with Welton Becket's personnel director, John McCartan. The Becket building was really in the center of things – at 5657 Wilshire Boulevard – right on the fashionable Miracle Mile.

When I met with Ralph and John, they suddenly realized it was time for the morning coffee break. I had never taken even a moment's break at Lynn-Western. Exiting the building, we went next door to the large, modern, sparkling Van de Kamp's coffee shop and bakery. There, we sat in a booth adjacent to an exterior wall of glass, watched the fashionable girls walking past, and ordered coffee and cakes. This was definitely different than Lynn-Western, where Norm once shouted at me for allowing the two secretaries to have a coke at their desks while they worked on a particularly hot day.

I was immediately offered the position of Assistant Director of Public Relations for Welton Becket and Associates. The salary offered was the same as I had been making – the now-fabled $600 a month. I accepted and Norm appeared shocked when I told him I was leaving after six trying months. And so began a most important and exciting change in my professional life.

Chapter Eighteen: Welton Becket and Associates, Los Angeles Architects

Los Angeles Moves West from Downtown

Joining Welton Becket and Associates, architects and engineers, was one of the best decisions I ever made and the firm had a major impact on my life -- opening my eyes to the world of architecture and interior design, to the amazing post-War evolution of Los Angeles and the United States as a whole, and to the complex world of commerce.

I began at Becket in July 1959 and my first office was literally a converted broom closet. But when my friend and now my boss Ralph -- who had only been on the job a month or so himself -- gave me a tour of the building, I was blown away.

Our public relations offices were in a two-story annex of the firm's main five-story building on Wilshire Boulevard, sharing the annex with the Interior Design Department. Thus, my tour began in Interior Design and I was not ready for the blast of color, texture and excitement that met me when we opened that door. Interior Design included interior design, interior decoration, graphic design and a Becket specialty -- department store design.

We walked past work stations festooned with carpeting, draperies, wall coverings, even dinnerware. One of the projects at the time was a restaurant in a planned department store in Denver, and some of the designers were wearing Persian costumes being created for the waiters, complete with shoes whose toes curled up at the point. A number of the interior designers were gay men, and they were chuckling with enjoyment of their work. Dan Morganelli was director of design and his chief assistant, Werner Heumann, was a Jewish immigrant from Germany.

An elevator in the hallway took us to the fifth floor of the main building where we walked past architectural designers sketching office towers, hotels, hospitals and shopping centers. Then we passed a sea of draftsmen working on construction drawings. And finally we went into the executive offices, elegant with blond woods and designer furnishings. Here, I met Welton Becket himself, a handsome, well-dressed, sophisticated, soft-spoken gentleman who welcomed me to the firm.

Included in my first day was an invitation by Mr. B, as we called him, to lunch in the executive dining room, which some called the "inner sanctum." Here, each day, Mr. B invited 11 guests to join him for a gourmet lunch prepared and served by a chef whom Mr. B stole from his wife who had originally hired the chef for the Beckets' Holmby Hills home, designed by the firm. The sprawling Becket home, just off Sunset Boulevard and adjacent to Bel Air, was across the street from the Holmby Hills home of Becket friend Walt Disney..

Welton Becket and Associates was one of four premier Los Angeles commercial architectural firms, and what I call "big-time" commercial architecture was highly competitive. We were competing with the firms of Periera & Luckman (which broke into two firms shortly after 1959), Victor Gruen and Associates, and Albert C. Martin.

Of interest, architects William Periera and Charles Luckman were both Jewish, Periera coming from the motion picture studios and Luckman from a management career at Lever Brothers. And Victor Gruen, a renowned land planner frequently called the father of the modern shopping center, was a Jewish immigrant from Austria.

But Becket, along with A.C. Martin, were the "establishment firms." Welton Becket belonged to the exclusive non-Jewish Los Angeles Country Club together with the heads of Los Angeles-headquartered insurance companies, corporations, newspapers, department stores and non-Jewish banks. And now the Becket firm's public relations was in the hands of two young Jewish men, Ralph and me.

Welton Becket and Associates, architects and engineers, pioneered the concept of "total design," in which a single firm did land planning, architectural design, working drawings including written specifications, interior design, interior decoration, and engineering – structural, electrical and mechanical. And everything was under one roof in Los Angeles, although at the time there were smaller Becket offices in San Francisco and New York City.

I learned that there were two types of architects, design architects and project architects. The design architects designed buildings. But the project architects were responsible for actually producing the buildings by heading a team which turned the design sketches into working drawings and written specifications; coordinating with civil, structural, mechanical and electrical engineering; and most importantly overseeing costs, timing and relations with the client.

Among the leading design architects in the firm was Louis Naidorf, a Jewish architect who had designed the circular Capitol Record building in Hollywood and the-then brand new Los Angeles Sports Arena.

At the Becket firm, depending on the type of project on which they worked, the project architects were guided by one of several coordinating architects specializing in office buildings, retail centers, hotels or hospitals. I had an especially close relationship with Harry Widman, a thoroughly professional Jewish coordinating architect who lived in the San Fernando Valley and was responsible for hospitals. The Becket firm had done the UCLA Medical Center and continued on a number of additional buildings in that complex.

The firm had been founded during the 1930s by Walter Wurdeman and Welton Becket -- Wurdeman being the main design architect. The young men won a competition for their design of the "streamline moderne" Pan Pacific Auditorium in Los Angeles; came to the attention of motion picture stars; and began designing motion picture stars' homes in Bel Air, specializing in rustic-modern wood and glass. Their modern residential designs caught the attention of the president of Bullock's, downtown Los Angeles' premier department store, who had a concept for a post-War residential-themed department store in the Los Angeles suburban city of Pasadena.

The resulting Bullock's Pasadena gained wide publicity, and the Becket firm was commissioned for Los Angeles' first two major post-World War II office buildings, each within the City's then 13-story height limit. Wurdeman and Becket designed the General Petroleum building in downtown Los Angeles, which established the concept of modular office building design, and the bold Prudential Insurance Company Western Regional Headquarters on Wilshire Boulevard, which floated on a concrete slab because of its adjacency to the La Brea Tar Pits.

When Walter Wurdeman succumbed to a sudden heart attack at an early age, the firm became Welton Becket and Associates.

By the time I joined Becket in 1959, it was a well-established, widely-heralded firm. The major excitement in the firm at the time was a coming move of the Becket office to a new building under construction as the first structure in a completely new master-planned multi-use complex planned by Becket and recently named Century City. Mr. Becket had personally selected the two architects for the firm's new building and both happened to be Jewish: Louis Naidorf as design architect and Alan Rosen as project architect.

Century City, developed on what was the back-lot of 20th Century Fox motion picture studios, had a major impact on the development of Los Angeles, and I was privileged to be a part of the planning and early development.

But there was another project that was even more intriguing. For years, Los Angeles hungered for a performing arts center, and several previous attempts at developing a center for symphony, dance, opera and light opera had failed. Finally, Mrs. Norman Chandler, wife of the publisher of the Los Angeles Times, stepped up and created an agreement with the County of Los Angeles to use a vacant seven-acre site in the Los Angeles Civic Center. Then she went to work raising the money.

Mrs. Chandler, at that time the reigning queen of Los Angeles society, had worked with Welton Becket and Associates on an earlier project -- a remodeling of the Hollywood Bowl -- and she took it on herself to commission the Becket firm to create the Los Angeles Music Center on the prominent downtown site, certainly every architect's dream.

I remember the day one of Becket's project architects whom I had not yet met, John Knight, returned to the office from an out-of-the-office joint venture to which he been assigned -- the new Los Angeles International Airport. I walked over to introduce myself to John, and on his desk in his small project architect cubicle were a few sheets of schematic drawings given to him by an architectural designer and labeled the Los Angeles Music Center. It was 1959, and during the ensuing eight years while the three-building Music Center was being designed and constructed, I got to know John, his project and downtown Los Angeles exceedingly well.

* * *

This was a period in the history of Los Angeles when downtown was barely hanging on – everything was moving to the west. The City's movers and shakers, essentially non-Jewish bankers, insurance executives and publishers -- who dined at Perino's restaurant on Wilshire Boulevard near Hancock Park, played golf at the Los Angeles Country Club on Wilshire near its intersection with Santa Monica Boulevard, and lived in the Hancock Park and Pasadena mansions -- were looking to the west.

And the mostly Jewish movers and shakers of the motion picture industry -- who dined at Chasen's restaurant on Melrose Avenue even farther west, who played golf at the Hillcrest Country Club near the 20th Century Fox studios, and who lived in Beverly Hills, Brentwood and Bel Air -- were already in the far westside of Los Angeles.

One of the defining moments in the City's history, keeping some life downtown, came when Los Angeles-headquartered Security Pacific National Bank, then the second largest bank in California after San Francisco's Bank of America, decided to keep its headquarters on Spring Street downtown. The bank had considered developing an entirely new building on Wilshire Boulevard somewhere between Vermont Avenue and Crenshaw Avenue in Mid-Wilshire or farther west along the Miracle Mile. But the decision was made to stick with downtown and to remodel the existing historic headquarters building on Spring Street, Los Angeles' historic financial center.

The Security Pacific National remodel was awarded to the Becket firm. In keeping with the post-War theme of efficiency, the floors surrounding the building's dramatic five-story central atrium were extended over the atrium, creating far more floor area but destroying the atrium. This was hailed at the time as a splendid use of wasted space, but today would bring down the wrath of the architectural and preservation communities.

* * *

For me, 1959 was an especially important year for three reasons. I joined the Becket firm, I had a minor operation removing a growth on my thyroid which was benign, and – wonder of wonders – on October 12 ,Tamar delivered us of a beautiful new baby girl, whom we named Judith Ann. To this day Judy enjoys my telling her how I felt – as if I were walking on air -- as I left the Kaiser Hospital on Sunset Boulevard. Judy was dark complected like me. Now I was the father of a daughter in addition to two sons.

These were great years for Los Angeles, for Los Angeles Jewry, for the Becket firm and for me and my family. Our expense account at the Becket firm was wide open, and Ralph and I entertained the press lavishly.

A man named Tom Cameron had become real estate editor of the Los Angeles Times, and every Sunday the Times had a giant real estate section resulting from all of the residential advertisements as the city blossomed forth. Yet, the real estate section editorially concentrated on commercial development, and the section had a huge amount of editorial space to be filled each week. As the largest and most important architectural firm in the City, we were able to provide a number of major articles every week, and were constantly featured.

In addition, we fed the city side of the newspaper with news of Los Angeles International Airport, the Music Center, Century City, and a vast number of new office buildings including the 21-story Travelers Insurance building in Mid-Wilshire, the first building to exceed the City's 13-story height limit.

Ralph and I lunched with news media and clients' public relations people during the day at the chic Windsor and Brown Derby restaurants near the Ambassador Hotel, and Tamar and I joined Ralph and his wife in entertaining the media at dinners in the evening at such star-studded venues as Mateo's in Westwood and Scandia on Sunset. In addition, Ralph and I would go to opening parties and events everywhere in the City, some to which we were invited and some which we crashed. Los Angeles was growing up, and everyone was celebrating.

In 1960, the Becket firm moved into its new five-level headquarters at 10000 Santa Monica Boulevard in what was to become Century City. The building had a bold exterior surrounded by a colorful tile mural, and motion picture studios as well as advertising agencies requested permission to use the exterior as a backdrop. The interior, especially the fourth floor offices, was breathtaking. Visitors would gasp as they exited the elevator on the fourth floor with its reflecting pool, fountains and textured walls. Our public relations offices on the third floor were spacious and modern, and I now had a grand office with a wall of glass overlooking the Los Angeles Country Club and the Beverly Hilton Hotel across Santa Monica Boulevard.

On the fifth floor was a luxurious cafeteria, with glass windows overlooking the entire Westside of Los Angeles. Here we took our coffee breaks, but we typically went out for lunch. Here we also had our company parties and the fabled Christmas parties – this was still a time when employers served huge amounts of cocktails to employees at company gatherings.

The development of Century City was a joy to behold as it rose next to our headquarters building. Twentieth Century Fox studios, like other motion picture studios during the late 1950s and into the 1960s, was on a decline. The corporate bosses determined that the 180-acre "back lot" adjacent to the sound stages was surplus and could be sold for monies that would bolster the failing motion picture business. However, the studio was located between Santa Monica Boulevard and Pico Boulevard in West Los Angeles, off of Wilshire Boulevard and west of the island city of Beverly Hills. Was this too far from downtown and from Mid-Wilshire?

The first plan which economic consultants gave to 20th Century Fox showed the land's potential use for light industrial. But studio head Spyros Skouras had bigger ideas. He retained the Becket firm whose planning department conceived of an entirely new mixed-use center encompassing high rise office towers, a hotel, a retail center and residential towers. The name given, in honor of Twentieth Century Fox, was Century City, to be bisected by a major thoroughfare called the Avenue of the Stars.

But finding a developer who wanted to buy the property was not easy. New York's fabled William Zeckendorf was finally interested and took an option to buy at $54 million, but could not find a financial partner. When he dropped out, developer Marvin Kratter, like Zeckendorf a Jew, made a stab, reduced the price to $45 million, then dropped out. At $45 million Zeckendorf returned and located an interesting partner, Aluminum Company of America – Alcoa. Alcoa, a Pittsburgh-headquartered aluminum manufacturing giant, saw Century City not as a real estate opportunity but as an opportunity to showcase aluminum in the buildings.

In line with the master plan, Becket designed the first two office towers – with skins of aluminum -- and the retail center. To Becket's dismay, the operator of the Century Plaza hotel, Seattle-headquartered Western International, insisted on a Seattle architect.

Time passed quickly, and on October 4, 1962, three years after the birth of Judy, Tamar and I had our fourth child, Marla Gail, again a beautiful daughter, but this time light complected like Tamar. For Marla's birth, after taking Tamar to the hospital, I went home – only to be called a short time later that we had another girl. Freshly shaved and showered, I returned to Kaiser Hospital, waved and smiled at the bleary-eyed fathers still waiting in the waiting room.

We were now the parents of two handsome boys and two beautiful girls, all three years apart. Our family was complete. Steven and Danny were attending Cowan Avenue elementary school, a highly ranked public school a few blocks from our house in the upscale Kentwood area of Westchester. And both enjoyed Saturday mornings at Temple Israel's religious school. Tamar was now teaching at the religious school and I enjoyed Saturday mornings at home with the girls.

And at work, the Los Angeles Music Center was nearing completion. Ralph and I were in the midst of doing public relations for one of the first post-War performing arts centers in the nation.

Chapter Nineteen: To Valencia and Back to Becket

The Music Center Downtown, Century City of the Westside

The Pavilion of the Los Angeles Music Center, later to be named the Dorothy Chandler Pavilion, opened in 1964 with great pomp. After the pre-opening press party, Tamar and I took the heads of the Los Angeles bureaus of the Wall Street Journal and the Associated Press and their wives to dinner at Perino's, the most exclusive restaurant in Los Angeles.

Opening night itself was white tie and tails, and Tamar and I attended as Zubin Mehta conducted the Los Angeles Philharmonic Orchestra on the first night in the orchestra's new home. The rest of the week was black tie, and we hosted press each night for dinner in the plush Pavilion restaurant atop the Pavilion before each performance.

Every large newspaper in the nation sent its theater critic to cover the opening, and we were besieged by requests from the wire services, television and radio stations, and newspapers all over the world. This was a public relations person's dream, and Ralph and I were living it.

Two years later, in early 1966, Los Angeles Times real estate editor Tom Cameron called me to say he had recommended me for a position as director of public relations for a new, master-planned community. When the call came from Norval LaVene, marketing vice president for a new community to be called Valencia in northern Los Angeles County, out of curiosity I accepted an invitation for an interview.

Norval was an interesting individual who had been a name partner in a large advertising agency. The Valencia brochure he showed me was colorful and intriguing, and the salary was $14,000 a year, 17 percent more than the $12,000 I was then earning. I accepted the position and shocked Ralph when I told him I was leaving.

A major drawback to my new position, which was with the California Land Company, a division of the historic Newhall Land & Farming Company, was the location. California Land was developing the new master-planned community called Valencia on the 44,000-acre Newhall Ranch in far northern Los Angeles County. My new office was a 50-minute high-speed drive by freeways from our home in Westchester.

However, the new community – master planned by Victor Gruen Associates – was slow in materializing and my new boss was pleasant but not ideal. It was here I met Thomas Nielsen, who moved up from chief financial officer to president of California Land; Peter Kramer, who was in charge of the planned industrial park; and a public relations consultant named Thomas Wilck. There were some pleasant moments, several public relations achievements, but in all I was not happy with my decision.

Fortunately, my long-time friend and former boss Ralph Jackson missed me terribly and succeeded in getting his boss, Jack Beardwood, vice president in charge of business development for Welton Becket and Associates, to call me 10 months after I had left and offered to match the $14,000 salary if I returned. I did not hesitate.

My return to the Becket firm in November 1966 was warm in every way. All of the architects greeted me with enthusiasm, and Welton Becket himself invited me to lunch with him and the other officers in the "inner sanctum" dining room the first day I came back. Moreover, Ralph had secured impossible-to-find tickets for the UCLA-USC football game. He had met a young lady who worked in the UCLA ticket department.

My family was also pleased that I once again had a 20-minute drive to work on city streets rather than the long drive on the freeways. At California Land, I had worked until 6:00 p.m. or longer most days, coming home at 7:00 p.m. or later. At Becket we charged out of the office at 5:00.

Our family life was most pleasant. Tamar always had the four children run to greet me with the shout "Daddy's home" every weekday evening when I returned from work, and we had lovely dinners together. On Sundays it was my turn to make pancakes, and I formed each of the children's initials with the batter.

We especially enjoyed our vacations every year. During a week in the summer we would go to San Diego's Mission Beach, where we at first rented a unit right on the beach at the Beach Cottages and in later years rented an entire little house a block from the beach. We spent the mornings on the beach and the afternoons on the bay. Then, for a week during the schools' winter vacation, we went to Desert Hot Springs just north of Palm Springs where we rented a large unit at the Sundial Terrace.

Our two-bedroom and small den, bath-and-one-half home in Westchester which we purchased in 1959 was getting small for our family. We began looking for a new home elsewhere, and we looked at Jewish West Los Angeles -- but Westchester, with Tamar's father's temple and our many friends, seemed to be the place to remain.

We made an offer on a four-bedroom, and gave a $500 deposit, only to realize a few days later that the square footage was too small and we decided to cancel. This resulted in the owner, a top executive with Hughes Aircraft, suing us after he sold it to the listing agent for less than we offered even though prices were escalating. We then had to retain an attorney, and after weeks of aggravation for us and for the former owner's wife, we settled.

Instead of looking for another house, we decided to add on to our existing home. Fortunately, we were referred to an excellent contractor and remodeled our home with great success. We enlarged the den and added a new wing with a master bedroom and bath. Thus, the boys had a room, the girls had a room, the den was used for fun, the children had their own bath and one-half, and we had our own bath.

We utilized Becket's extensive interior design and decoration library of materials and catalogues to obtain special finishing materials and draperies, and shopped for them with an interior decorator's discount along interior designers' rows on Robertson and Beverly Boulevards.

Returning to the Becket firm, I went to work again on such projects as the Music Center's next two buildings, the Mark Taper Forum and the Ahmanson Theater. Originally, Mrs. Chandler, who spearheaded the entire Music Center project, would not accept donations of over $25,000 from any person so as to have a more democratic fund-raising campaign

But now, to meet the fund-raising goal for the $33.5 million project, she accepted a $1 million naming gift from Jewish savings and loan tycoon Mark Taper for a circular theater we had called the Center building, and that became the Mark Taper Forum. Polish-born Taper came to the United States from a successful retail background in England and settled in Long Beach, California. Through a series of events, he became a home builder and developed thousands of homes in the area, particularly in the southern Los Angeles County community of Lakewood. His next venture was to found First Charter Financial Corporation, which became a major Los Angeles-headquartered savings and loan firm.

The savings and loan industry was highly competitive. So, because Mrs. Chandler accepted a $1 million naming gift from Taper, she then had to accept the same from rival savings and loan tycoon Howard Ahmanson, founder of the giant Home Savings & Loan. And thus came into being the Ahmanson Theater, the third of the three theaters making up the Los Angeles Music Center. In later years, the largest building, the Pavilion, was named for Dorothy Chandler.

Interestingly, several excellent job opportunities came my way shortly after I returned to the Becket firm in late 1966 as

Ralph's assistant director of public relations. I was offered head public relations positions with sizeable increases in salary from a growing homebuilder headquartered in Westwood Village; with a huge construction firm in San Francisco; and with the Jewish-sponsored Cedars-Sinai Hospital in West Los Angeles.

The concept of working for a homebuilding developer – even though the firm was headquartered in Westwood Village – made me somewhat uncomfortable, so I turned down that position. In later years, that firm, owned by the Jewish Jerry Snyder, became one of Los Angeles' largest real estate developers. And moving my family to San Francisco for the position with the construction firm was out of the question, although the person who accepted the position with Bechtel Corporation became one of the highest-paid public relations executives on the West Coast.

But I was tempted by Cedars-Sinai. I met with the director of development who had called me, and at the meeting he showed me a faded copy of the elaborate fact sheet I had written for the Music Center. He asked if I knew who had put it together. When I answered that I had, he smiled, admitting that this is what he had been told.

Five years earlier, the Jewish-sponsored Cedars of Lebanon Hospital had merged with the Jewish-sponsored Mount Sinai Hospital to form Cedars-Sinai, and the combined hospital was about to develop a major new medical center on Beverly Boulevard near La Cienega Boulevard.

He offered $16,000 a year, $2,000 more than I was making, and with all Jewish holidays off. However, I felt that I could not possibly leave the Becket firm after having just returned and told him, really as an excuse, that the salary was insufficient. He called back the next day, saying the hospital administrator was ready to offer me $18,000. I had to thank him, but confessed that I could not leave my current employer.

Three years later, I was truly happy with my decision to remain with Becket. The years had been good ones, the projects were broad including work at UCLA, my alma mater, and Century City -- where we sometimes had lunch at the 20th Century Fox commissary -- continued to emerge. Moreover, by this time I had an excellent assistant.

We were working on a book about the firm which was to be published by McGraw-Hill and we thought we were about to get commissioned to design Security Pacific National Bank's new skyscraper planned atop Bunker Hill in downtown Los Angeles.

Our founder, Welton Becket, had divorced his wife and was dating the widowed Mrs. Walt Disney. I even went along on a date to see the circus at the Becket-designed Los Angeles Sports Arena because it was covered by the news media. We had a spectacular cover story on Mr. B and the firm in Business Week, followed by a major article in Fortune magazine. And then, in 1969, at the age of 66, Mr. B had a sudden heart attack and passed away – a shock to the entire firm.

With Welton Becket's passing, the position of president was taken over by his nephew, MacDonald Becket. Don, who was my age, 41 at the time, had graduated in architecture from the University of Southern California, had worked as a project architect in the firm, and was now in business development.

Don had bold new ideas for the firm, including a major national expansion.

My friend and boss Ralph grew disenchanted with Don's goals and made contact with rival architectural firm Charles Luckman, which had some years earlier broken off from the firm of Periera and Luckman. The Luckman firm had recently made a radical change by allowing itself to be absorbed by the giant conglomerate Ogden Corporation to form Ogden Development and thus entered the field of real estate development as well as architecture.

Ralph was offered the position of director of public relations for the Ogden firm, located in a bold, black office tower on Sunset Boulevard between the Sunset Strip and Beverly Hills. And he arranged his new position so that he could bring me along as his assistant.

While I liked Ralph as a friend, I was not interested in continuing as Ralph's assistant, and did not want to leave the Becket firm. Our boss, Jack Beardwood, came to my office, told me Ralph was leaving – which I knew – and told me that Ralph said he was taking me with him. He asked me whether I was going to leave. I told him decidedly not. He punched my shoulder and told me that I was now director of public relations of Welton Becket and Associates.

Chapter Twenty: Becoming a Vice President – the Golden Years

The San Fernando Valley Exerts its Attraction

The years from 1969 to 1973, during which I served as director of public relations and then as vice president of public relations for Welton Becket and Associates, architects and engineers, were by most measures the most fulfilling, most fun, and most fantastic years of my working life. Don Becket, now president of the firm, did have highly aggressive expansion plans in mind and carried them out.

Moreover, probably foolishly, we worked without a budget. I had an unlimited expense account and regularly exceeded it. I once asked Don for a budget, telling him that I did not know whether I was spending too much money or not. His answer: "Martin, I will tell you when you are spending too much money, and you are not spending nearly enough yet."

All air travel within the firm was first class, at a time when there were no frequent flyer miles, and all of our fellow passengers were corporate presidents, Hollywood celebrities and millionaires. We had a corporate apartment in New York City in the East 70s which occupied the entire floor of a brownstone, and in time acquired a corporate apartment on the 77th floor of the John Hancock Tower in Chicago, which the firm's interior design department furnished and decorated beyond belief.

When not in a corporate apartment, we stayed only in the finest hotels, dined in every city's most exclusive restaurants, entertained lavishly, and held executive gatherings at the nation's most outstanding resorts. Don even purchased a mansion on Lake Arrowhead, a resort two hours from Los Angeles, which was used by Becket executives for rest and relaxation.

Don enlisted me as his most trusted confidant and I was a nearly daily guest in the "inner sanctum" dining room, making up the invitation list myself when Don was out of the office.

Expansion came rapidly. In addition to our headquarters office in Los Angeles, we had an office in San Francisco which was enlarged from smaller quarters on Maiden Lane to a full floor in the bold Crocker Plaza building we designed on Market Street. Our New York office was moved from a partial floor in the Colgate-Palmolive Building on Park Avenue to a full floor of a tower on 59th Street just off Park Avenue. And we greatly enlarged our Houston office which occupied its own building near downtown.

Then we acquired an architectural firm in Chicago and an architectural firm in Atlanta, enlarging each and making them Becket offices. To further expand our capabilities, we acquired structural, electrical and mechanical engineering firms in Chicago, New York and Atlanta.

My public relations staff was also enlarged. I inherited one professional and two secretaries when I became director and added four more professionals in Los Angeles and one in New York.

I amazed myself in two ways. First, I took over two jobs that Ralph had begun and I completed – a book on the Becket firm entitled "Total Design" which was published by McGraw-Hill, and a successful campaign to acquire for Don Becket the coveted title of Fellow in the American Institute of Architects, FAIA.

Secondly, as assistant to Ralph, I was the quiet and steady writer and hard worker somewhat behind the scenes, allowing Ralph to provide the sometimes required pushiness frequently attributed to a public relations leader. Now I took on some dash.

Following a groundbreaking for a Shell Oil Company land development project called Plaza del Oro in Houston, both the assistant to the governor of Texas and an assistant to the president of Shell Oil complained to Don that I was too pushy at the events on behalf of the architectural firm. Don told me about the complaints and we laughed our heads off on the flight home, as we poured over the Houston Post and Houston Chronicle which featured photos of Don and not of the governor nor the Shell president.

My relationships with the business and real estate press throughout the nation grew immensely, partly because of my membership in the National Association of Real Estate Editors (NAREE) to which Glenn Fowler, the real estate editor of the New York Times, nominated me. For example, I arrived in Houston a day early for the Plaza del Oro groundbreaking, sought out fellow NAREE member Charlie Evans – the renowned real estate editor of the Houston Chronicle – at the bar in the Houston Press Club at the Rice Hotel, and then visited with NAREE member Carl

Hooper, the real estate editor of the Houston Post, at his office. The rest was easy.

My media contacts also grew with the national publications headquartered in New York City – Time, Business Week, Fortune and the architectural magazines. And what fun I had with Glenn Fowler of the New York Times, who became a personal friend.

The New York Times in those days devoted its Sunday real estate section to commercial real estate, and Glenn used many of my articles regarding projects around the country. When I was in New York, we dined together at lunch and at dinner in the finest restaurants. And when Don Becket and I hosted a party for real estate editors during a convention in Chicago, Glenn led a huge continent of the nation's top real estate editors to our John Hancock building apartment, walking from the Chicago Hilton hotel.

My relationship with clients was also strong. On a visit to Boston to call on the news media, I would call on our corporate and developer clients and once invited them to come to a special party in our New York apartment, resulting in a large attendance of distinguished clients that amazed both Don and the head of our New York office.

Don also told me I was working too hard, usually traveling on Sunday so I could be in a city on a Monday. "Fly on company time and take your wife with you when you can." Shortly after that offer, Tamar and I flew first class on TWA to Washington, D.C. with actor Jimmy Stewart and his wife across the aisle. In Washington we stayed in a magnificent suite in the Watergate Hotel, where we entertained those members of Tamar's family who lived in Washington. On another occasion, we held a family party in the Becket firm's lavish New York City apartment for the large family contingent Tamar had in that city.

In 1972, with the national economy slowing and perhaps in place of a salary increase, I was elected a vice president – the only non-architect in the company to hold that title. Following that appointment, I lobbied Don, without success, to give a vice presidency to my best friend in the firm, John McCartan, the long-time personnel director. John and I frequently went out to lunch together.

The vice presidency gave me new stature among the media, the clients and our own staff. I could walk into the San Francisco, Chicago, Atlanta or New York offices and the office director would hang on my every word, knowing how close I was to the president. My visits to the New York office always concluded with cocktails in the director's office with the director and several of the head architects, then a walk to the Running Footman for another cocktail or two with the director, a walk to the director's east 50s apartment for a cocktail with him and his wife, and finally we went out to cocktails and dinner with media or clients at Lutece or Sign of the Dove.

At home, there was a major transition. My father-in-law, Rabbi Soloff, had turned 72 and his congregation – now called Temple Jeremiah after a merger with a small Reform congregation in adjacent Inglewood -- was not growing. Temple Jeremiah's lay leaders decided it was time for a change and they asked the rabbi to retire. He did so, but with great disappointment.

This changed Temple Jeremiah for us, but we remained active members, Tamar being co-president of the Sisterhood and head of the Temple's gift shop. Several rabbis succeeded Rabbi Soloff, but none suited the congregation for long.

Part of the Temple's lack of growth resulted from waning Jewish population in the area, which affected both Temple Jeremiah and the Conservative Westchester Jewish Congregation which had a synagogue on Manchester Avenue. Some residents were uprooted by the taking of homes for the expansion of Los Angeles International Airport, but others moved to the more Jewish parts of Los Angeles as their children approached dating age.

Then there was some exodus from the fashionable community of Ladera Heights, adjacent to Westchester, which was undergoing ethnic change. Ladera Heights was developed during the late 1950s and 1960s by the Los Angeles Investment Company. The unincorporated land extended from Slauson Avenue on the north to La Tijera Avenue on the south and on both sides of La Cienega Boulevard. Unlike the pre-war homes and immediate post-war homes in Westchester -- which were small and had front living rooms -- the Ladera homes were sprawling one-story homes with the new center hall plan.

Ladera Heights homes were priced in the $40,000 range, considerably more than the $26,000 we had paid for our second home in the somewhat-exclusive Upper Kentwood area of Westchester. Although the South Bay was not considered an especially Jewish area, Ladera Heights attracted Jewish doctors and other professionals who had practices in the South Bay area.

All Ladera Heights school children were enrolled in the adjacent City of Inglewood school system. But Inglewood, once a middle-class Caucasian suburb, which years before had anti-Jewish restrictions, was changing as African-Americans moved west from South Central Los Angeles. As the Inglewood schools became more heavily African-American, many of the Ladera residents began sending their children to private schools and others left the area.

We were delighted that two couples who moved from Westchester to Ladera Heights and whom we count among our closest friends from the days of the Young Marrieds at Temple Israel of Westchester, Jack and Nikki Gold and David and Edith Ostrove, remained in Ladera Heights. Jack, a physician and originally from Boston, had moved with Nikki to the area to join a Westchester medical practice; and David, an attorney who grew up in Los Angeles and Edith moved to the area for the family-friendly neighborhood.

However, in 1972, two families who are among our closest friends decided to move to the San Fernando Valley. Richard and Maureen Sherman decided to move to a more Jewish community. Dick Sherman had come to Los Angeles from North Carolina to get his doctorate degree in history from the University of Southern California and Maureen had come from cold Winnipeg, Canada to pursue a nursing career in warm Los Angeles. They met and married in Los Angeles and moved to Ladera Heights to be closer to El Camino College, where Dick was a professor.

For the Shermans and their growing family, the Jewish environment of the San Fernando Valley was a draw, and the

Shermans decided to move there. Following a Friday night service at the Temple, Dick asked me where in the San Fernando Valley they should locate.

I did not really know the Valley well, but I told him that I understood the best part of the Valley was considered to be south of Ventura Boulevard. I also told him that I thought once- heavily Jewish Sherman Oaks, directly east of the San Diego 405 Freeway, was getting old and played out, and that Jews were moving west. I said that Encino, directly west of the 405 Freeway was highly Jewish but expensive. So, I reasoned that the next community to the west, Tarzana, would be ideal – south of Ventura and protected by Encino from blight.

I was surprised when, at a Temple board of directors meeting the following Monday, Dick told me that the Shermans had bought a home in Tarzana, "just as you said." They did buy, in a lovely and heavily Jewish area called Braemar.

The other family to move, Peter and Marian Schwartz, moved because of job relocation. Peter, an aeronautical engineer, was one of many young Eastern professionals who were attracted to Los Angeles from New York in the 1950s by the growing aerospace industry. So many of these young couples came from the East during those years that whenever I met a new young couple at our Temple on a Friday evening, I would ask "Are you from New York or Chicago?" And they were surprised that I had guessed. Then I would ask the husband "Are you working at North American Aviation or at Hughes Aircraft?" And again they were surprised that I knew.

Like the others, Peter Schwartz and his young wife, Marian, had left family and friends in New York and moved to Los Angeles where Peter accepted a position with Hughes Aircraft in the Westchester area.

But now Hughes relocated Peter to its Canoga Park missile facility in the San Fernando Valley. The Schwartz family had been living in Westchester-adjacent Culver City in a garden-like two-story condominium. This was the first any of us had ever heard of a condominium and we were certain it would be impossible to sell. But it did sell quickly, and the Schwartz' moved to the increasingly Jewish West Hills section of the Valley.

Remaining in place was another of our close friend couples, Harrison and Lee Weitz. They had moved from Oregon to Los Angeles for a job opportunity and bought a home in Hawthorne, just south of Westchester. They continued to live in Hawthorne as that once-quiet community developed exciting technology and retail centers.

The year 1972 was also a big one in that our elder son, Steve, graduated from Westchester High School and entered college. He applied to and was admitted to UCLA, moved into a residence hall on campus, and I began to make out the first of many, many checks to the Regents of the University of California. Our son Dan was then in Westchester High School and in later years would go to UCLA; our elder daughter Judy was in Orville Wright Junior High School and would also go the UCLA; and our daughter Marla was in Cowan Avenue School and would likewise go to a University of California campus, but in Santa Barbara..

In early 1973, with the nation in one of its recessions, I finally received a raise in salary at Welton Becket and Associates – five percent, bringing me to $23,000 a year. In addition, I typically received a Christmas bonus of about $3,000. The previous Christmas, in addition to the regular bonus, I received a special check for $500 from Don, for the help I gave him in his position as Honorary Counsel General to the Republic of Ceylon in Los Angeles.

And after the office Christmas party during which bonuses were handed out, Don invited me into his office for a personal drink with him, with his top executive vice president Furman Myers, and with Don's cousin, Bruce, who was a project architect and owned part of the company. I was really an insider.

But things were no longer totally joyous at the firm. Bruce, the son of founder Welton Becket, was critical of how his older cousin, Don, was running his late father's company, and some of the resulting problems came my way as I became an intermediary. Shortly after the Christmas party, Bruce sued Don and Don fired Bruce. With troubles within the firm and with the miserly salary increase, even with my unbelievable expense account, I decided it was time to look elsewhere.

Chapter Twenty-One: A Changing Los Angeles

Forced Busing and Immigration Affect the Jewish Community

A significant impact to the peaceful existence of the Los Angeles Jewish community resulted from a 1963 legal decision, Crawford v Board of Education of Los Angeles, which required the Los Angeles Board of Education to come up with a plan for desegregation of schools by 1977. The court order was in reaction to what was considered to be unequal education, in which African-American students living mainly in the south-central parts of the city were educated in nearly all-Black schools.

Following the court's decision, I had attended a session devoted to school integration during a national biennial convention of the then-Union of American Hebrew Congregations (UAHC), the Reform Jewish movement's blanket organization. During that session, I stood up and forecast that – as justified as the court's decision might be – the result would have a devastating effect on the Los Angeles Jewish community, and called upon the UAHC . for some plan of action – which never came.

The desegregation plan devised by the Board of Education was to bus a proportion of the African-American students from south-central Los Angeles to essentially all-Caucasian schools on the west side of Los Angeles and in the San Fernando Valley. To add to the proposed integration, a portion of the Caucasian students in all-white schools in those areas would be bused into schools in south-central Los Angeles.

The result, as might be anticipated, was two-fold: white flight from the Los Angeles Unified School District to adjacent school districts, and white flight from the public schools to a group of hastily established private schools. To an extent, this flight to private schools resulted in a more-rapid development of non-Orthodox Jewish all-day schools.

As Los Angeles became increasingly urban, and especially after the 1992 "Rodney King Riots" which flared out of south-central Los Angeles and onto the near west side of Los Angeles, some Jewish families relocated southward to new communities in adjacent Orange County. However, in most cases those who moved to Orange County were mainly attracted to the area because their professional careers – medical, financial, legal – took them there.

But to the greatest extent, the westward movement of the Los Angeles Jewish community continued to dominate. The Jewish people moved to the far western segments of Los Angeles' San Fernando Valley – to Woodland Hills and West Hills; then farther west to the relatively new cities of Calabasas and Agoura Hills, which are still in Los Angeles County but are served by the highly desirable Las Virgines School District. And they moved even farther west to adjacent Ventura County into the communities of

Westlake Village and Thousand Oaks. And then even northwest into the once desolate Simi Valley.

At the same time, upscale African-Americans were leaving the south-central ghetto, especially as legal and illegal Hispanic immigrants began to multiply within the formerly all-Black ghetto. The African-American movement was westward into formerly all-Jewish areas as well as into the eastern counties of Riverside and San Bernardino. On the west side of Los Angeles, formerly nearly all-Jewish high schools such as the fabled Fairfax High and Los Angeles High became populated with African-American students.

As the Fairfax area became more urban, Orthodox Jews began concentrating into the long-time Jewish area around Pico Boulevard and Robertson Boulevard known as Pico-Robertson. Today, along Pico Boulevard especially, shop after shop boasts of Kosher products and restaurants.

Ironically, a second Orthodox concentration evolved in what was once the heavily Waspish area of Hancock Park, closer to the center of Los Angeles. Here are large, individually styled homes – mansions actually – once the neighborhood of Los Angeles' elite gentile bankers, insurance moguls, corporate executives and publishers. Today, Orthodox families can be seen walking to local synagogues which have sprung up, sometimes outraging non-Orthodox neighbors, in homes throughout the community.

A major impact on the Los Angeles Jewish community during the last decades of the 20th Century was the changing world-Jewish situation.

First came young travelers from Israel, who traditionally travel the world after their required Israeli army service. Once they witnessed the beauty, the weather and the economic possibilities offered by Los Angeles, they remained. And they communicated to their friends in Israel that they had discovered a true paradise – so their friends and relatives came, legally and illegally.

The Los Angeles Israelis formed a bond, provided employment and resources for one another, and remained essentially as an island unto themselves, typically not associating with Jewish synagogues nor communal organizations. The Israelis tended to concentrate in the San Fernando Valley, where most prospered.

Next came the Russian Jews when the Soviet Union finally permitted Jews to leave. A large segment of the Russian Jews were without financial resources, and for a period they were a favorite charity of the Southern California Jewish community. The Russian Jews tended to concentrate in the section of West Los Angeles which was later incorporated as the City of West Hollywood.

Another Jewish influx were the South African Jews, who left South Africa as conditions there changed. These Jews were English speaking and those who came to Southern California flocked to Los Angeles, to the Irvine area of Orange County, and into the La Jolla area of San Diego County. Although the South Africans had to leave much of their assets behind, they came with sufficient funds, excellent education and tremendous entrpreneurial drive and typically became successful as they integrated into the greater Jewish community.

Finally came the Iranian Jews. The Iranians, in seemingly greater numbers than the Israelis, Russians and South Africans, were generally extremely well off financially. In Los Angeles, they concentrated in the upscale Westwood area south of UCLA and in the City of Beverly Hills. In Orange County they concentrated in upscale Newport Beach and Irvine.

Typically extremely observant, the Los Angeles Iranian Jews discovered a home in Temple Sinai, the large, Conservative congregation on Wilshire Boulevard between Westwood and Beverly Hills. They also developed their own large congregation in the San Fernando Valley.

To catch up with their congregants, the synagogues also moved west. Today, there are in excess of 120 synagogues in the Los Angeles area, including Chabad and some small Orthodox establishments.

Although the giant, Reform Wilshire Boulevard Temple retains its magnificent 1928 Byzantine home in the mid-Wilshire area near Western Avenue, where for generations its late senior rabbi Edgar F. Magnin dominated Los Angeles Jewry, the Temple now operates a satellite facility on Olympic Boulevard in west Los Angeles. Still, the Temple plans to invest millions of dollars to improve its historic facility with the concept that younger Jews are moving back to the currently heavily Korean mid-Wilshire area.

Moving to the westside decades ago was the large, Conservative Temple Sinai, which relocated from the mid-Wilshire area to a massive complex on Wilshire Boulevard near Westwood Village. Shortly thereafter, the large Sephardic Temple Tifereth Israel moved to a dramatic complex just down the Boulevard which is now lined by expensive, high-rise condominiums.

Of special note is the gigantic Reform congregation Stephen S. Wise. Rabbi Isaiah Zeldin, formerly senior rabbi at the lovely Reform Temple Emanuel in Beverly Hills, left and formed Stephen S. Wise, placing it strategically atop the Santa Monica Mountains between heavily Jewish west Los Angeles on one side and the heavily Jewish San Fernando Valley on the other. The result is that Stephen S. Wise became one of the largest Reform congregations in the entire nation.

Somehow, it is impossible to write about any Jewish location in the world and not at least mention the delicatessens. During the 1930s and 1940s, Cantor's on Brooklyn Avenue in Boyle Heights in east Los Angeles was the place. Cantor's made the move west to Fairfax Avenue in the 1950s and the large restaurant, with its bakery and deli counter, is still a favorite of many. Remaining in the once-Jewish area of Westlake Park, just west of downtown, is Langer's on Alvarado Street near Wilshire. Langer's still rates high, especially for its pastrami.

In west Los Angeles, Junior's on Westwood Boulevard just off Pico Boulevard is a long-time favorite. And, of course, there is Nate 'n Al's in Beverly Hills, where it is still possible to see motion picture celebrities and Jewish billionaires munching on corned beef sandwiches. There are several other delicatessens in west Los Angeles, including in the Pacific Palisades and adjacent Santa Monica, but none stand out.

When it comes to Jewish delicatessens, the San Fernando Valley seems to dominate. Most Los Angeles Jews will agree that the tiny Brent's, in the west Valley and always crowded, is tops. And now Brent's has opened a second, larger store in Westlake Village, following the Jewish population all the way west to the Ventura County border. Still, the long-time Art's in Studio City has its advocates, with the Studio City area of the eastern part of the Valley still heavily Jewish.

Chapter Twenty-Two: Farewell to Los Angeles

To the Suburbs and the Adjacent Counties

For the adventure of it, and disappointed with my salary at Welton Becket and Associates, in early 1973 I answered an advertisement in the Los Angeles Times for a public relations director at a real estate development firm.

Unknown to me, the advertisement had been placed by Tom Wilck, who had just taken the position of vice president in charge of public affairs for The Irvine Company, a huge land owner, developer and real estate manager. Also unknown to me was that the firm was headquartered in Newport Beach, a city in Orange County – the rapidly growing county directly south of Los Angeles County.

Tom knew me from the days his public relations firm consulted at Newhall Land & Farming Company when I was there in 1966, and in subsequent years when we consulted together while his firm represented The Equitable Life Insurance Company, for whom the Welton Becket firm had designed a 38-story building on Wilshire Boulevard. And on Tom's invitation I had once joined the public relations advisory board of a Los Angeles non-profit organization for which his firm consulted.

Tom called me to meet him. Although I had no intention of really leaving my secure position at Becket, I told him that I had a reason to come to Newport Beach. Becket was doing an addition for The Irvine Company to the Becket-designed Fashion Island shopping center, and I wanted to see the progress.

When I got there, Tom showed me the elaborate public affairs organization he had just inherited, including departments of public relations, community relations, government relations, marketing, advertising, two publications, and a television station. The public relations director position was vacant and Tom said he needed me to fill it.

Tom had earlier folded his Los Angeles public relations consulting firm in order to join the Richard Nixon administration in Washington, D.C. as head of communications for the Small Business Administration. When Nixon's first term ended in 1972, Tom decided to return to California and joined The Irvine Company to head the public affairs department just left vacant by the dismissal of its former head.

I told Tom that I could recommend some candidates. He smiled and said, "I don't want any recommendations, I want you." He did not delay in offering me the position of director of public relations. The salary, he thought, would be $30,000 plus a bonus – a 30 percent increase over what I was making at Becket. But I told him that a relocation from Los Angeles to Newport Beach was out of the question.

On returning home, I told Tamar that I had just seen an opening for an excellent position at a really nice salary with an important company, and that I was going to recommend some people.

"Would you be interested in taking it?," she asked.

"We wouldn't want to move to Orange County," I answered.

"But isn't it pretty down there?," she inquired.

"Well yes," I said, and let it go at that.

The next day, I received a telephone call from The Irvine Company's personnel department. The caller wanted to explain the offer: $28,000 to start with $2,000 more in six months; a 10 percent bonus potential; a savings plan where the company invested 50 cents for every dollar you invested; a pension plan; a company-provided automobile including all gasoline and service; membership in two country clubs; an excellent medical program; and a key to the company's private beach.

It was a hard package to turn down. I indicated that I might be interested. Tom called the following day and asked me to meet William Mason, president of the company. The opportunity to meet Mason, a significant figure in Southern California land development, really appealed to me, and I drove down on a bumper-to-bumper Friday afternoon along the San Diego Freeway.

Although I arrived late, Tom got Bill Mason out of a meeting for a moment and Mason greeted me in a side office. We quickly discussed the company and my background, and I told him what I could do for the company public relations-wise regionally and nationally, where few knew of the firm. I mentioned Fortune and

Time magazines, Business Week, the New York Times and the Wall Street Journal.

"Never mind those publications, we need you to get control of the local Daily Pilot newspaper," he said, and left. The next Monday, Tom called and officially offered me the job.

My loyal secretary at the Becket firm, Gail Wells, who transferred to me the several previous calls from The Irvine Company, asked bluntly whether I was going to join that company. Gail sensed everything. A week later, I made the decision and told Don Becket I was leaving. He instructed me not to do a thing, telling me that the Becket firm would match the salary. But the next day he told me that he had spoken with Furman Myers, the senior vice president for administration, and they determined that since I was currently earning the same salary as the top architectural designers, increasing my salary was impossible.

By this time I was committed to joining The Irvine Company and I gave the customary two-week notice with a letter of resignation. Nearly anyone else leaving the Becket firm departed for another architectural firm, a competitor, so the administration did nothing at their departure. However, I was not leaving to join a competitor but rather was joining a potential client, so I was treated warmly. Don invited me into the executive dining room for a farewell lunch and I was given a rousing goodbye party at Senor Pico's, a favorite Century City restaurant.

And so, in May of 1973, I began the 50-mile commute from my home in Westchester to Newport Beach. In 1973, there was still little traffic going to Orange County in the morning and returning from Orange County in the evening because residents of Orange County typically worked in Los Angeles County, so my drive took only 50 minutes in what was a "reverse commute.". Moreover, the Watergate hearings were going on in Washington, so I was glued to the car radio. In a few weeks I was provided with a company car and company gasoline, which made the drive highly economical.

In time, I realized, we would be moving to the Newport Beach area, so I began to investigate any Jewish presence. I knew that there was a Reform Jewish temple called Harbor Reform. Harbor Reform, with Rabbi Bernie King, met in a church but had an office in the marine-oriented Lido Village area of Newport Beach. I visited the office and asked the three women working there whether I could have a membership list, to determine in which sectors of Orange County the Jewish people lived. I received the same erroneous answer that I have received in cities all over the nation – "They live all over."

However, one woman said that there was a map on the wall with a pin indicating the location of each member's residence. Looking at the map, I called the women over and pointed out several large concentrations of pins – the Mesa Verde area of the adjacent City of Costa Mesa, in which even the rabbi lived; the University Park area of the adjacent City of Irvine, in which the new University of California, Irvine, campus was located; and along several streets in the Westcliff area of Newport Beach, where the doctors lived so they could be convenient to Hoag Memorial Hospital.

A year later, we sold our home in Westchester for $58,000 and moved into a lovely, four-year-old, four-bedroom-and-den and three-bath home on Catamaran Drive in the Harbor View Hills area of Newport Beach for which we paid $95,000. We found 10 Jewish neighbors on the street, including a Jewish neighbor on either side of our home.

And thus it was that in 1974, I left my life-long position as a Los Angeles Jew and officially became an Orange County Jew.

Epilogue

My parents, Jack and Revella Brower, sold Brower Sheet Metal in 1976 and my father retired at the age of 80. Although the shop was located in south-central Los Angeles, near the infamous community of Watts, my father's building was spared during the 1965 Watts riots. My father was later told that the word was out to spare the old Jewish man's building – "he is a good guy."

Some years before my father retired, my mother discovered that the street on which they lived, Hi Point near Pico Boulevard and Fairfax Avenue, had been re-zoned from single-family to multi-family. Working with a contractor, she had the house on Hi Point demolished, and with a mortgage based on the land -- which by then my parents owned -- she developed a seven-unit apartment house. My parents occupied the front unit and rented the other six.

Based on the success of that venture, several years later my parents bought a four-unit apartment house on the more exclusive Shenandoah Street, west of La Cienega Boulevard, and eventually moved into one of those units. Retired, and with income from the apartments and from interest on the proceeds of the sale of the shop, my parents spent most days at the Century Plaza shopping center in Century City. There they met with other Jewish seniors and lunched nearly daily at Clifton's Cafeteria, then a part of the shopping center.

The heavily Jewish area in which they lived became what some considered less safe in the early 1980s, and as my parents aged, it was determined that they would be safer if they lived nearer to my sister Diane and my brothers Erwin and George in the San Fernando Valley. They sold the two apartment houses and then, with a substantial savings account paying the high interest of those years, moved to an apartment complex on Reseda Boulevard in Northridge. There they spent many hours at the Northridge Fashion Center and became familiar with several restaurants in the area.

My father passed away a day before his 87th birthday in March of 1983. My mother remained in the apartment with a live-in assistant until her passing in March of 1989.

* * *

Tamar's mother, Eve, was a true real estate maven. She had built a triplex in the upscale Ladera Heights area adjacent to Westchester, and Tamar's parents occupied the large owner's unit. She had wanted to purchase a vacant corner lot on Manchester and Airport Avenues, but was discouraged by real estate professionals. That lot became the site of a large telephone company building.

Bitten by the real estate bug, Eve encouraged a friend to buy an eight-unit apartment house on 79th Street in Westchester, but her friend deferred. So in 1962 Eve bought the building with the consent of her husband, Rabbi Soloff, on the condition that Tamar and I would manage the building. And so we did. When Eve passed away in 1980 followed by Rabbi Soloff in 1992, we

– together with Tamar's brother Rav who lived in the East -- inherited the apartment house. The $70,000 apartment building, purchased with $13,000 down, is now managed for us by a management firm and provides a generous monthly income.

After the passing of Eve, Rabbi Soloff lived alone until his death at the age of 91. His former congregation, Temple Jeremiah, continued to lose members as Westchester's Jewish population aged and moved away, and the Temple was merged with Temple Akiba in adjacent Culver City. There, Rabbi Soloff became rabbi emeritus. He continued to write books, traveled and even took a one-year position as rabbi in Perth, Australia, when he was in his eighties.

* * *

Our eldest child, Steven, was at UCLA when we moved to Orange County. He graduated and immediately entered UCLA Law School, complaining that he had been going to school ever since pre-Kindergarten at the Temple. He passed the State Bar on his first try and joined a law firm in the Encino section of the San Fernando Valley. Steve married Carol Heston, a "Valley girl," a banker in Encino, and after a time of living in the west Valley, to our delight Steven joined an Orange County law firm and moved to Orange County. Steve and Carol have two of our grandchildren, Stephanie and Jason. They live in the Nellie Gail Ranch area of Orange County and Steven is a successful attorney with a prestigious law firm.

Our second child, Dan, had to adjust to moving to Corona del Mar High School in Newport Beach from Westchester High School for his senior year when we moved to Orange County. An outstanding athlete, he made the adjustment when he found he could play AYSO soccer until the age of 18 rather than the 15-year-old cutoff in Los Angeles. Dan also graduated from UCLA, decided he did not like advertising after a year with a Hollywood agency, and on our suggestion visited my brothers Erwin and George at a high-tech firm called Teledyne in Northridge. Dan married Kate Porter, a legal secretary living in North Hollywood, and is now director of software engineering at Teledyne Controls. They live in Calabasas in the far west San Fernando Valley. Kate has a grown daughter, Lisa.

Judy, our third child and first daughter, entered Corona del Mar High School as a freshman. She was active on the student newspaper, graduated from UCLA in communications, interned during vacations at the local Daily Pilot newspaper and on graduation joined a public relations firm in Newport Beach. Following successful associations with two other public relations firms, she opened her own public relations firm and represents clients in real estate, retail and entertainment. Now located in Irvine, the firm is named Brower, Miller & Cole – the Miller for Tamar's mother's maiden name and the Cole for my mother's maiden name, Kolochinsky. She is married to Charles Fancher, a real estate developer, and they live in Newport Beach.

Marla, our fourth child, entered Lincoln Middle School in Newport Beach when we moved to Orange County. She later graduated from Corona del Mar High School and decided to attend the University of California, Santa Barbara – being favorable to UCSB since we all had spent a week there at a UC summer camp when she was a child. She graduated in psychology from UCSB, forming lasting friendships, and returned home to Newport Beach. At home, through a series of events, she entered the field of homeowner association management. She married Mark Hemmel and together they have their own homeowner association management firm, BHE Management Corporation, headquartered in Laguna Niguel. They have one son, our third grandchild, Mason, and live in the Monarch Beach section of Orange County.

* * *

We travel to Los Angeles frequently because that's where my sister and brothers continue to reside.

The Freedmans, my sister Diane and her husband Jack, caused great consternation to my mother when they decided to move from west Los Angeles to the San Fernando Valley in the 1960s. Jack had taken a computer programming job with a firm called Teledyne which had relocated to Northridge, and Jack and Diane found a new home there. The house they found was in a new development called Princess Estates near Nordhoff and Louise Streets – 3,000 square feet on one floor set on a half-acre lot for $55,000. My mother did not want them to move to the "far off" Valley nor to spend that kind of money – homes near her were only $26,000.

But move they did, and their home has become the entertainment center for our extended family for any number of occasions, Diane being the perfect hostess. Diane and Jack have three daughters and a son, all married with children. Three of the families live in the San Fernando Valley, the other in the East.

My brother, Erwin, with a strong electronics background, worked in medical electronics at such institutions as John Tracey Clinic in Los Angeles, then joined our brother-in-law Jack at Teledyne in Northridge. On joining Teledyne, he moved with his wife, Ellen, from a home in the highly Jewish Beverlywood section of Los Angeles to the community of Chattsworth in the San Fernando Valley.

Erwin's marriage to Ellen is a family story. Ellen Soloff is Tamar's first cousin. While on a week's vacation from nursing school in Boston, she stayed with Tamar's mother. My mother-in-law asked me if one of my brothers would take her out on a date. Erwin did and we captured another Soloff into the family. Erwin and Ellen have two sons, both married with children. One son lives in the San Fernando Valley, the other in Northern California.

My brother George stayed single the longest and was able to enjoy the new singles lifestyle which entered the American scene in the late 1960s. After working in our father's shop following his stopping out of UCLA, he graduated from California State University, Northridge – commonly known as CSUN and because of its west Valley location extremely Jewish. While attending CSUN, he moved to the San Fernando Valley from our parents home and took his own apartment – a new trend for its time. Following work in a highly advanced-for-its-time global positioning firm, he joined Jack and Erwin at Teledyne in Northridge.

Earning a good living and single, George drove a new Cadillac Eldorado and used an interior decorator to furnish a large apartment. George finally married Kathy, who was somewhat younger and with whom he enjoyed skiing. George was the only one of us five Browers to marry non-Jewish. George and Kathy had a daughter and a son, and moved to Denver where George took an important job and where Kathy's parents resided. But in time George and Kathy divorced, after which George contracted Hodgkins lymphoma and passed away in 2002 at the age of 66.

My brother Gary worked in our father's shop, Brower Sheet Metal, until the shop was sold and my father retired. Gary then purchased a bakery supply delivery business and serviced bakeries throughout the Los Angeles area until he retired. Gary married Rita Lowy, who kept the books for medical professionals, and they have two sons, both living in Los Angeles. When not traveling somewhere in the world, Gary and sometimes Rita, who live in the long-time Jewish neighborhood near Fairfax Avenue and Third Street, go nearly daily to The Grove, the exciting new "lifestyle" retail and entertainment center adjacent to the Farmers Market, one of Los Angeles' endearing sightseeing locales.

* * *

Our combined families have developed a Los Angeles tradition over a period of many years of visiting all of our deceased parents at Eden Memorial Park in the far north San Fernando Valley. Although my grandparents and uncle Sam are buried in the Home of Peace, the old Jewish cemetery in east Los Angeles just east of Boyle Heights, all of our relatives after that are buried at Eden.

Every March, because that's the month when both of my parents passed away, we first visit the graves of my parents, there remembering our brother George and several cousins. From there we walk to the graves of the Freedmans, my sister Diane's husband Jack's parents, who moved to Los Angeles from New Jersey to be near their grown children. And there we also remember Jack's sister Annette.

Next we go to the graves of the Soloffs, my wife Tamar's parents, and Tamar translates for us the Hebrew gravestones. Nearby we find another set of Soloffs, my brother Erwin's wife (and Tamar's cousin) Ellen's parents, who moved to Los Angeles from Fall River, Massachusetts, to be near Ellen. Finally, we visit the graves of the Lowys', my brother Gary's wife Rita's parents and uncle, who moved to Los Angeles with Rita from Cleveland (and originally with Rita from Rumania).

At each stop, we talk about the lives of our departed parents and relatives and then recite the Jewish prayer for the departed, the Kaddish.

* * *

Tamar and I have now been a part of Orange County, California for the past 34 years, including a close involvement with Jewish Orange County. During this time I was an intimate part of The Irvine Company, the County's largest developer and landlord, for 12 years; then together with Tamar we published a monthly subscription newsletter called "Orange County Report" for 15 years. Since then I have written a weekly column called "Along the Coast" for Coast magazine, which circulates along the gold coast of Orange County. During this time I have also written two books and many articles on Orange County. And I have taught public relations in the evening at the University of California, Irvine, and at California State University, Fullerton.

We became an integral part of the Jewish community, from our 34-year membership with Reform Temple Bat Yahm in Newport Beach to our participation in the founding of Heritage Pointe, the Jewish Home for the Aging. I served as president of the Orange County chapter of the American Jewish Committee, which honored us, and then our entire family was honored by Jewish Family Service. And I have been active in the Orange County Jewish Historical Society.

But the story of the development of the Orange County Jewish community will have to wait for my next book: Orange County Jew.

* * *

During the last years of the 20th century and the first years of the 21st, Los Angeles as a city underwent a major change in leadership. As insurance companies such as Pacific Mutual Life left for Orange County; as the huge Los Angeles-headquartered banks such as Security Pacific and First Interstate were absorbed by other banks; as the local department store chains such as Carter Hawley Hale, Bullock's and Robinson's were absorbed by national chains; as the powerful Los Angeles oil companies such as Atlantic Richfield, Union Oil and Getty were absorbed; and as even the Los Angeles Times was purchased by out-of-state interests, Los Angeles lost its gentile civic leaders.

Into the gap has come a single Jewish leader, Eli Broad. Broad, whose Los Angeles-headquartered Kaufman & Broad homebuilding firm and a subsequent insurance company made him a billionaire, has led a Los Angeles cultural and commercial renaissance and is perhaps the single most important civic leader in the city. Although leadership of the motion picture and television industry in Hollywood has remained essentially Jewish, these leaders have traditionally kept to themselves.

Among political leaders, Los Angeles is represented by numerous Jewish U.S. Congressmen, re-elected regularly from the Jewish communities. And the powerful five-member Los Angeles County Board of Supervisors includes Jewish activist Zev Yaraslovsky, representing the west side, of course.

Thus, during the 80 years since my birth in Los Angeles in 1928, the city has become a Jewish stronghold, both in size of population – the third largest in the world – and in diversity and power.

Throughout the centuries, people have always wanted to live in a Mediterranean sub-tropical paradise. In Los Angeles and Southern California, they have found it.

The End